PHILOSOPHY IN THE
TRAGIC AGE OF THE GREEKS

Philosophy in the Tragic Age of the Greeks

FRIEDRICH NIETZSCHE

Translated, with an Introduction by
MARIANNE COWAN

A GATEWAY EDITION
Regnery Publishing, Inc.

Copyright © 1962 by Regnery Publishing, Inc.

1998 printing.

Library of Congress Cataloging-in-Publication Data

Published in the United States by
Regnery Publishing, Inc.
An Eagle Publishing Company
One Massachusetts Avenue, NW
Washington, DC 20001

Distributed to the trade by
National Book Network
4720-A Boston Way
Lanham, MD 20706

Printed on acid-free paper.
Manufactured in the United States of America

10 9 8 7 6 5

Books are available in quantity for promotional or premium use. Write to Director of Special Sales, Regnery Publishing, Inc., One Massachusetts Avenue, NW, Washington, DC 20001, for information on discounts and terms or call (202) 216-0600.

PHILOSOPHY IN THE
TRAGIC AGE OF THE GREEKS

INTRODUCTION

I

The sixth and fifth centuries in Greece were a proving ground as well as a primal ground for Nietzsche's philosophy. Like so many thinkers before him, and a few since, Nietzsche saw in this period an incomparable golden age in which the human spirit flowered in an abundance greater than men have since known. Further, he was of the opinion that even during this, their best period, the Greeks fell short of complete fulfillment of their self-evident potentialities. Nonetheless they achieved a more magnificent culture, if also a more spectacular and thought-provoking failure, than any other culture available for our observation. So Nietzsche believed, and he also believed that they would continue to merit the contemplation and study of untold generations. "The Greeks have surely never been overvalued," [1] he wrote early in life, and from that estimate he never wavered.

[1] X, 237. (III, 348). The first citation here and others throughout this introduction refer to the volume and page of the old Naumann edition (*Gross* or *Kleinoktavausgabe*) of Nietzsche's works (*Nietzsche's Werke*, Leipzig, 1894ff). The second citation, in parentheses, where given, refers to the most recent edition: Friedrich Nietzsche, *Werke in drei Bänden*. Ed. Karl Schlechta; Carl Hanser Verlag, München, 1954ff. It was unfortunately not possible to cite this later edition in all instances since not all of Nietzsche's early notes have been republished in this otherwise much superior edition.

1

Nietzsche's judgment of the Greeks rested in part, naturally, on a long European tradition, and on good rational historical interpretation of his time.

> So much depends on the development of Greek culture because our entire occidental world has received its initial stimuli from it. An adverse fate decreed that the late and decadent forms of Hellenism should exert the greatest historical force. On their account, earlier Hellenism has always been misjudged. One must know the younger Greece in great detail in order to differentiate it from the older. There are very many possibilities which have not yet been discovered because the Greeks did not discover them. And others have *discovered* the Greeks and later *covered them up* again.[2]

This fragment from one of Nietzsche's early notebooks shows that he, in considering the Greeks, was by no means devoid of a sense of historical balance, not even during his most worshipful period. Nonetheless, much more than historical judgment is involved in his concern with them. He seems to have had an intuitive certainty, resting on a numinous, incontrovertible source in his own being, that the Greeks had achieved the highest type of culture that the world had seen. "Indescribable riches were lost to us," [3] he felt, when their culture perished. They hold for him "all the eternal types," [4] as well as the "archetypes of philosophical thought," as he calls the pre-Socratic philosophers. But, dearest of all, they are the collective representa-

[2] X, 219. (III, 335).   [3] X, 230. (III, 342)   [4] X, 143.

tives of the eternal intuitive type, the discoverers
of "the beautiful possibilities of life." [5]

It is his instinctive reliance upon his own unconscious bases, plus the frequent intuitive emergence into self-recognition, that lends to Nietzsche's utterances, here as elsewhere, such an ir-
idescent, if not maddening twilight of contradic-
toriness. We feel anything and nothing may be
seen by its glow, and as we are lured by it into
one blind alley after another, our affectivities
begin to explode. During the same period in
which the foregoing quotations were written
Nietzsche exclaimed: "How can one possibly
glorify and laud a whole people!" [6] Again, he
characterized this same "whole people" as "lacking sobriety and suffering from excessive sensi-
bility, from abnormally heightened nervous and
cerebral activity." [7] Disturbed, we give vent to
our irritation in line with our own seemingly rational temperament. Some close the book altogether, others delete from conscious memory one
of the apparently contradictory viewpoints of
Nietzsche (often arguing the more heatedly in
favor of the one retained); still others enjoy with
unholy glee the apparently irresponsible behav-
ior of the "mad" philosopher.

The Nietzschean incongruities, however, are
the peculiar pitfall of the Nietzsche devotee and
may scarcely be felt by the less interested reader
who knows Nietzsche, largely by reputation, as
the great iconoclast among philosophers. Such a
reader may well wonder that the "breaker of old
tablets," and "transvaluor of all values," should

[5] X, 234. (III, 345).   [6] X, 384.   [7] X, 387.

have acquiesced so peacefully in the century-old traditional values ascribed to the ancients, as is evidenced by the little essay entitled "Philosophie im tragischen Zeitalter der Griechen." And such wonder is quite justified, even beyond the immediately apparent. For although Nietzsche's treatment of the Greeks seems to us today to fit into an unbroken, if gradually extended, tradition, this was by no means the opinion of his contemporaries. Had this essay been published, it might well have had for its audience an effect as electrifying as *Die Geburt der Tragödie aus dem Geiste der Musik,* which Nietzsche published in 1872. *The Birth of Tragedy* presented a view of the Greeks so alien to the spirit of the time and to the ideals of its scholarship that it blighted Nietzsche's entire academic career. It provoked pamphlets and counter-pamphlets attacking him on the grounds of common sense, scholarship and sanity. For a time Nietzsche, then professor of classical philology at the University of Basle, had no students in his field. His lectures were sabotaged by German philosophy professors who advised their students not to show up for Nietzsche's courses.

"Philosophy in the Tragic Age of the Greeks" [8] came from the same period of Nietzsche's thinking. It is necessary to know that the work as it is here published was never completed. It occupies a place in the posthumously published voluminous notes and fragments. Nevertheless it is different from the bulk of these notes in that

[8] On the translation of the title see below, page 19.

Nietzsche had a clean copy of it made, within a year or two of its writing, and refers to it as the manuscript of a new whole book, albeit one far from completion. Various plans for completion are also extant, none comprising more than a paragraph or two, as well as jottings consisting mainly of the names of the pre-Socratic philosophers followed by various key-words of characterization. In addition, serious study of the essay in question demands some acquaintance with Nietzsche's concurrent plans for other (also not completed) books on related topics, notes and fragments of which add up, at present, to several hundred printed pages.[9] Taking all this into consideration and leaving out, for the moment, the matters covered in the published *Birth of Tragedy,* one may safely hazard some general suggestions about the fundamental objectives which Nietzsche hoped to advance through the essay here translated.

Nietzsche's most deeply felt task at this time was undoubtedly one of education. He wanted to present the culture of the Greeks as a paradigm to his young German contemporaries who might thus be persuaded to work toward a state of culture of their own; a state which Nietzsche found sorely missing.

To get past Hellenism by means of deeds: that would be our task. But to do that, we first have to know what it was! There is a certain kind of thoroughness which is but the excuse for

[*] An authoritative edition of this segment of tne notes and plans is still lacking. See footnote 1, above.

inactivity. Think of what Goethe understood
about antiquity: certainly not as much as any
philologist, and yet quite enough to enable
him to engage in fruitful struggle with it. One
should not, in fact, know more about a thing
than one can oneself digest creatively. More-
over the only means of truly understanding
anything is one's attempt to *do* it. Let us try
to live in the manner of the ancients—and we
shall instantly come a hundred miles closer to
them than with all our learnedness. Our philologists nowhere demonstrate that they somehow strive to vie with antiquity; that is why
their antiquity is without any effect on the
schools.[10]
My aim is to generate open enmity between
our contemporary "culture" and antiquity.
Whoever wishes to serve the former must
hate the latter.[11]

To this end Nietzsche apparently tried to com-
pose at least two books, one dealing primarily
with philosophers; the other to concern philologists. The connection of the latter with his fundamental aim is easily seen. Philologists hold
most intimately and immediately in their hands
the legacy of Greece. On their work, pious or
pioneering according to their individual temperament, depends the image of Greek culture in
the minds of present and future generations.
However, Nietzsche's book about philologists was
never written; plans for it are mingled with
plans for the one on philosophers, and both are
partly absorbed in various of his *Thoughts Out
of Season,* a group of essays, four of which
[10] X, 410.   [11] X, 352. (III, 329).

Nietzsche completed and subsequently published.[12]

Perhaps the basic reason for Nietzsche's inability to write the work on philologists was the fact that he was himself one. The problems lay too close for perspective; they were an ever-present irritation.

> I enquire now as to the genesis of a philologist and assert the following:
> 1. A young man cannot possibly know what Greeks and Romans are.
> 2. He does not know whether he is suited for finding out about them.
> 3. And above all, he does not know whether, even with his information gained, he is suited to being a *teacher*. In other words, what determines him is not insight into himself or into his science but rather:
>   a. imitation,
>   b. inertia (he continues to do what he has been doing at school),
>   c. and eventually the intention to earn his livelihood.
>
> I think that 99 out of 100 philologists *ought not* to be such.[13]

It appears that Nietzsche did not believe that he was among the one in a hundred. Classical philology had failed to open itself to him as a distinct vocation. He knew early in life that as the possessor of a many-sided and expansive temperament, he would have to quite consciously

[12] *Unzeitgemässe Betrachtungen.* I (1873) ; II-III (1874) ; IV (1876).
[13] X, 344. (III, 323f).

choose a proper profession. It would have to be one which might make use of certain fundamental interests and inclinations, and at the same time, involve as few as possible of many envisioned evils. He knew also that he would undoubtedly regret his choice, whatever it turned out to be, as having been too confining for his intuitive temperament. As he foresaw, so it was. Yet he remained a professor of classical philology for ten years, retiring only when a multitude of physical symptoms, among them near-blindness, forced him into the full realization that his time was up and that more urgent potentialities were pressing to live themselves out in him.

One extended quotation from the philology-complex of his notes may stand here as typical of his approach to the problems that he recognized and experienced in this profession.

Let us imagine that there are free and superior minds who are dissatisfied with the liberal education (*Bildung*) that is now the fashion, and let us further imagine that they have summoned it before their court. What would the defendant's reply be? Above all, it would run like this: Whether or not you have the right to accuse anyone, in any event do not address yourselves to me but to my educators (*Bildner*), those who have fashioned my image. It is their duty to defend me, and I am privileged to keep silent, being nothing but their creation.

And now the educators would be lined up, and among them would be seen an entire profession: the *philologists*. This class consists, in the first place, of people who utilize their knowledge of Greek and Roman antiquity in order to educate the youth between the ages of thirteen and twenty and, second, of those whose task it is to see to it that there is an ever-renewed supply of such educators. . . . If now the state of liberal education of a given period is condemned, the current philologists are un der heavy attack. For either they perversely want the wretched condition of liberal education because it looks good to them as it is, or else they do not want it but are too weak to carry out the improvements the need for which they recognize. In other words, their guilt lies either in their deficiency of insight or else in their impotence of will.

In the first case their defense would be that they don't know any better, in the second, that they cannot do any better. But since philologists are educated primarily by the aid of Greek and Roman studies, the . . . deficiency of their insight might first express itself in their lack of understanding of antiquity, or second, in their unjustified comparisons between their own time and antiquity. They claim antiquity to be the most important aid to education, but it may be that antiquity does not educate at all, or at any rate, not any longer. If, on the other hand, one accuses them of impotence of will, the philologists might be fully justified in ascribing to the study of antiquity the educative significance and force that they do, but they themselves would obviously not be suitable instruments by means of which antiquity could exert this educative force. In other words, it would be wrong for them to have become teachers and they would be living in a false position. But

how did they get into this position? By being
deluded about themselves and their proper
vocation.

In order, therefore, to apportion to the philologists their proper share in the current bad
state of liberal education, one might sum up
the various possibilities as regards their guilt
or their innocence as follows:

*For the philologist to demonstrate his in-
nocence, he must have an understanding of
three things: antiquity, the present, and himself. His guilt lies in failing to understand
antiquity or the present or himself.*[14]

These words hint clearly enough that Nietzsche did not exempt himself from his various
attacks on the evils of the philological profession.
As is evident elsewhere, he felt in his maturer
judgment that he, too, had not succeeded as a
philologist, notably by failing to understand
himself. When Nietzsche decided that philology
as a life-work would suit him well enough, he
underestimated his scope, overestimated his endurance as an educator, and had not yet found
his ultimate tasks. Here, then, is one fundamental reason why the various fragments under dis-
cussion never saw completion.

It is still necessary, however, to look at the
other grouping of notes, those on philosophy and
philosophers, in order to come to a fair estimate of the problems hidden in "Philosophy in
the Tragic Age of the Greeks." To assay even
partially Nietzsche's views of the proper tasks of
philosophy would obviously be far beyond the

[14] X, 421ff. (III, 330ff).

scope of these remarks. The most that shall be done is again to select a sampling of the various threads left to us in the posthumous notes, threads that went into (or were noticeably left out of) the essay. They unravel rather freely to reveal two perennial concerns not only of Nietzche but of philosophers in general. They might be summed up in the two questions, "What are the functions and uses of philosophy?" and "What are the prominent features of the men who engage in philosophy?"

In Section 3 and in other scattered passages of the essay, Nietzsche discusses in general terms what he takes at this time of his life to be the functions of philosophy. It seems clear that he identifies philosophical thinking with intuition, scientific thinking with reasoned thought, and takes these two functions to be complementary to each other, though, as well, often temporarily opposed. In a number of unutilized notes and fragments, the most frequently occurring term for what philosophy does is *Bändigung*—which might be rendered "restraint" or even "taming." Thus as art tames the unbridled human instinct for knowledge, so philosophy restrains the religious instinct which is opposed to analysis and which seeks a single whole in which nothing is distinguishable. Again, philosophy tames mythical elements by strengthening man's desire for objective truth as over against free inventiveness. On the other hand, with the usual quick dialectic reversal of viewpoint, Nietzsche sees the pre-Socratic philosophers as out of season with their philosophy and thus, like all philosophers whom Nietzsche values, as fighting against the taming and restraining influences of their contemporary culture. "One may present these older philosophers as men who felt the Greek atmosphere[15] and mores to be constraining and limiting, hence as self-liberators." [16] The paradox is resolved in Nietzsche's over-all view of the philosopher as mediator between the equal spiritual dangers of boundedness and boundlessness. Thus, viewed from the side of science, myth may be looseness of thinking and idle invention; from the side of art, it is culture and creativity. It remains for philosophy to assay justly the position of myth at any given time and to support or counteract it, as needs be. This need not mean, to Nietzsche, a simple relativizing of opposites. The "taming" which he says philosophy is, may just as well consist of a denial that certain opposites are valid. Thus, "My general task: to show how life, philosophy and art may have a profound relationship to one another without philosophy being shallow or the life of the philosopher filled with lies." [17] Likewise he speaks of the false opposition between *vita practica* and *vita contemplativa*.

The philosopher then, above all else, is timely by being untimely. He counteracts far more than he acts, and thereby acquires, both justly and unjustly, the reputation for alienation and exclusiveness and general maladjustment to the

[15] I have followed the older edition here which reads *Luft und Sitte*. Schlechta has *Lust* which looks as though it might be a typographical error. If not, it might be translated as "pleasures."

[16] X, 222 (III, 337).   [17] X, 222. (III, 337).

human race. Philosophy, very much like lion-taming, is both an art and a science. It demands both heroism and know-how. It plays its role in the very midst of the human circus, with a strong element of the theatrical intrinsic to it, but it is a lonely business all the same. With such a view of philosophy it is easy to imagine how Nietzsche saw its practitioners. We may best follow him by looking at his portraits of them in "Philosophy in the Tragic Age of the Greeks." There remains but a word to be said on the incompleteness of the gallery. Nietzsche delineates in turn Thales, Anaximander, Heraclitus, Parmenides and Anaxagoras. Pythagoras he mentions in passing; his plans to include Democritus and Empedocles never ripened. One explanation for his inability to proceed may be his drawing too near to the figure of Socrates. "I understand the earlier philosophers as being the *forerunners of a Greek Reformation* but not as forerunners of Socrates. Their reformation never eventuated. With Pythagoras it remained sectarian. . . . Empedocles is the *great Reformer who failed.* When he did not succeed, only Socrates was left." [18] But "everything about Socrates is wrong." [19] The problem Nietzsche called "Socrates" remained an insuperable obstacle to him throughout his life. And even among the early notes there is one which reads, "Socrates, let me confess it, is so close to me that I am almost constantly doing battle with him." [20] This complex of problems has been dealt with at length in the Nietzsche literature and cannot be

[18] X, 223. (III, 337).   [19] X, 103.   [20] X, 217. (III, 333).

recounted here. There is another thread, however, one leading backward from the writing of our essay as well as far forward toward *Zarathustra* and beyond, that we may follow for a little while in order to gain some insight into the abrupt ending of the pre-Socratic gallery. To understand it, we must recall briefly certain major problems that Nietzsche had raised in his earlier work, *The Birth of Tragedy from the Spirit of Music.*

As the title indicates, Nietzsche examines the historical, philosophic and mythological sources of the Greek dramatists. Typically, he assumes that where there was such unprecedented clarity and splendor there must also have been dark, equivocal ground on which such blossoms could have flourished. And he finds a two-fold rooting of Greek tragic art represented by the Greeks themselves in what he takes to be their two basic art-deities: Dionysus and Apollo. Dionysus releases frenzy and orgy, wild panic music, drunken revelry and rhapsodic rhythms. He symbolizes mankind's urge to shed itself of human individualities and personalities, to submerge or resubmerge in a single all-embracing current of libido. Apollo stands for measure, form, civilized order. He expresses the principle of individuation. His art consists of a dream-like series of visual images that do not ask for the observer's total commitment. His genius is plastic and architectonic, rather than musical and moving. Alone, Apollo produces a Homer; together with Dionysus, with each informed and transformed by the other's godhead, they produce the "spirit of tragedy" as recorded by Aeschylus and Sophocles.

It is clear that Nietzsche does not present Dionysus and Apollo as historical creations, nor even as mythical deities. When he describes music as creating the tragic drama for itself in order to experience itself, he is obviously invoking archetypal configurations. Needless to say this was not at all understood by the critics of his day and it is indeed debatable whether we are in a position, even yet, to understand fully the import of the methodology Nietzsche here experimented with. This despite the fact that his categories "Dionysian" and "Apollonian" have found wide acceptance as describing cultural patterns far remote from the boundaries of Greek culture.

One obvious defect *The Birth of Tragedy* shares with "Philosophy in the Tragic Age of the Greeks" is fairly easily ignored in our day, though it seemed of crucial importance to Nietzsche's contemporary audience. This is the constant slanting of the two works to glorify the achievements of Schopenhauer and, in the case of *The Birth of Tragedy,* of Richard Wagner. Public controversy has stopped raging about the worth of Wagner and Schopenhauer. The propaganda that Nietzsche makes for them may seem to us unfortunate for the craftsmanship of his own work, but understandable and forgivable as an eagerly hopeful attempt of the young academic to practice what he preached: the philosopher's and philologian's task to further the fruitful and to attack the sterile in his own culture.

But we were seeking a more inward connection between *The Birth of Tragedy* and "Philosophy in the Tragic Age," one which might cast some light on the fragmentary state in which Nietzsche left the latter. In the earlier work Nietzsche had dealt with massive segments of myth, not only presenting them but adding to them, expanding them into a monumental landscape which he was the first to behold. Then came the counter-viewpoint. *Los vom Mythos*: Away from myth, was now his slogan as he prepared to write about the first philosophers who stepped beyond the confines of myth. The *tertium quid* that mediates between these opposites is again hidden in his notes, or rather continued in them from some initial hints recorded in *The Birth of Tragedy*. "The last philosopher," he calls it. This figure rises, ghost-like, behind the first philosophers whom Nietzsche, on the surface, describes so enthusiastically and optimistically. Who is this shadow-figure?

> *The philosopher of tragic insight (Erkenntnis).* He restrains the uncontrolled drive toward knowledge, but not through a new metaphysic. He does not set up a new faith. He feels the vanishing of the metaphysical ground as a tragic event and cannot find a satisfying compensation for it in the motley spiralling of the sciences. . . . One must willingly accept even illusion—therein lies the tragedy.[21]
> Tragic resignation. God knows what sort of culture it will yield! It begins from the back end! [22]

[21] X, 118f.   [22] X, 179.

Thus Nietzsche characterized the ghost that disturbed and fascinated him. It is the shadowy counterpart of Socrates, the optimist; Socrates who believes that to know the good is to do it. But Nietzsche, offspring of generations of Christian preachers, believed that to know good is also to know evil, and to know good and evil is a fatality. By a most interesting coincidence, (Freud in Vienna being but a few decades away), Nietzsche named this shadow "Oedipus." In *The Birth of Tragedy* he had explained or at least hinted at what Oedipus meant to him: the wisest of all men who, having solved the riddle of the Sphinx, i.e., having known and imparted the deepest secret of nature, the secret to which man is the answer, is punished by falling into the profoundest pit of unnatural involvement. (It probably takes post-Freudian insight to point out the further dialectic, namely that the crime against nature in another sense is the most "natural" thing in the world.) Oedipus, who has seen and experienced what was evidently not meant for man, who had blinded himself to man's limitations in nature, must blind himself in the living flesh when he reaches ultimate self-insight. Influenced by Freud, we think of Oedipus as the young man, hell-bent on his abysmal venture; Nietzsche's thought was of the old man who lived to see the venture's consequences. The "terrible solitude of the last philosopher" [23] is the image that held Nietzsche in its grip, even as he wrote about Thales emerging from mythical darkness and Heraclitus cherishing his proud aloofness.

[23] X, 146.

The last philosopher I call myself, for I am
the last human being. No one converses with
me beside myself and my voice reaches me as
the voice of one dying. With thee, beloved
voice, with thee, the last remembered breath
of all human happiness, let me discourse, even
if it is only for another hour. Because of thee,
I delude myself as to my solitude and lie my
way back to multiplicity and love, for my
heart shies away from believing that love is
dead. It cannot bear the icy shivers of loneliest
solitude. It compels me to speak as though I
were Two.[24]

This is not a passage from *Zarathustra*; it is one
of the jottings that did not reach "Philosophy in
the Tragic Age of the Greeks." But its icy breath
is present there and it overshadows Nietzsche's
conscious intention to paint with a few bold
strokes the portraits of the pre-Socratic philosophers. It may not have been Socrates, after all,
whom he did not care as yet to face. It may have
been the "failure" of Empedocles, the next philosopher to be taken up, that invoked the terrible mirror-image Nietzsche calls "the last philosopher," an image he was not ready to assimi-
late into himself.

II

All relationships between human beings involve choices and hence compromises with at-
tendant guilts and griefs. This truism has a particularly poignant significance for the translator
of a dead man's work, for one's partner cannot

[24] X, 147.

talk back. The feeling that one may have victimized or overpowered him can never be satisfactorily resolved. This delicate trouble area is something that the reader, too, shares in and should remain conscious of. The translation here offered should present no great obstacles to the reader's understanding, but some few points, as is usual, should be noted.

The greatest trouble was presented by the title, *Die Philosophie im tragischen Zeitalter der Griechen.* That ought of course to be translatable by any first semester German student as "Philosophy in the Tragic Age of the Greeks." But what can "The Tragic Age of the Greeks" mean in English? The "Greek Age of Tragedy"? Or an age which for some reason was an especially tragic one for the Greeks? Or both? We have two plans for prefaces by Nietzsche. Neither touches directly upon the point in question, but both emphasize that the book is to be an account of certain personalities, rather than a handbook of philosophic doctrines or the history of a certain period in philosophy. This suggests, not too remotely, that the philosophers are dealt with as though they were tragic heroes, or at least heroic figures in a time that was presented upon the world stage as a tragic drama. At the end of the first chapter, Nietzsche speaks of these philosophic personalities in the following words:

> When [the philosopher] . . . appears in the sixth and fifth centuries, among the enormous dangers and temptations and increasing secularization, walking as it were out of the cave of Trophonius straight into the midst of the

lavish luxuriance, the pioneer freedom, the
wealth and sensuality of the Greek colonies,
we may suspect that he comes, a distinguished
warning voice, to express the same purpose of
which the Orphic mysteries hint in the grotesque hieroglyphics of their rites.

And so it becomes clear that for Nietzsche the
Age of Tragedy was indeed a tragic age. He saw
in it the rise and climax of values so dear to him
that their subsequent drop into catastrophe (in
the persons of Socrates-Plato) was as clearly fore-
shadowed as though these were events taking
place in the theater.

It should further be noted that certain Greek
terms used by Nietzsche were left as they stand in
the original; notably *physis, hybris, logos,* and
nous. With the possible exception of *physis* (the
natural order of the universe), they are as familiar to modern English readers as they are to
Germans, though it must not be forgotten that
like the naturalized "chaos," "cosmos," and
"atom," they should be interpreted, so far as
possible, in terms of a context often quite different from the modern one.

A few other words which might also conceivably have been used in their Greek form to mini-
mize misunderstanding were used in German
translation by Nietzsche and, following him, are
used in English translation here. The important
ones are *apeiron,* the "boundless" of Anaximander, rendered by Nietzsche as *Das Unbes-
timmte* and as "the indefinite" here; *genesis* and
its various derivatives rendered by Nietzsche as
Werden, and in English as either "coming-to-be"

or "becoming," neither wholly satisfactory. Nietzsche also used *Geist* as interchangeable with *nous*, and it was accordingly here translated by "spirit," rather than "mind" or "intelligence" which some readers might expect to be more customary English equivalents of *nous*.

Finally, attention should perhaps be called to the fact that Nietzsche's quotations are here translated as they stand in the text, with quotation marks where Nietzsche placed them. It must be understood, however, that these are not necessarily correct citations from the ancient texts; in fact they almost never are. Thus when Nietzsche writes, "Thales said, 'not man, but water is the reality of all things,'" this is not a citation from any extant source of Thales. It is Nietzsche's way of emphasizing the significance of Thales' doctrine that water is the source of all things. It is not difficult nowadays, however, for the lay reader to check for himself the carefully translated and annotated texts of the philosopher in question, though he will do well to compare several such sources. For Nietzsche was certainly not the last classical scholar who has discerned in these texts certain prominent features of his own soul's landscape.

MARIANNE COWAN

PREFACE

So far as outsiders are concerned, we are satisfied to know their aims, accepting or rejecting them *in toto*. But in the case of people close to us, we judge them according to the methods with which they pursue their aims. Often we may disapprove of their aims but love them because of their ways and the nature of their intentions. Now philosophical systems are wholly true for their founders only. For all subsequent philosophers they usually represent one great mistake, for lesser minds a sum of errors and truths. Taken as ultimate ends, in any event, they represent an error, hence are to be repudiated. Many people disapprove of all philosophers because philosophers' aims differ too much from their own. They are outsiders to one another. On the other hand, whoever rejoices in great human beings will also rejoice in philosophical systems, even if completely erroneous. They always have one wholly incontrovertible point: personal mood, color. They may be used to reconstruct the philosophic image, just as one may guess at the nature of the soil in a given place by studying a plant that grows there. "So this has existed—once, at least—and is therefore a possibility, this way of life, this way of looking at the human scene." The "system" is a growth of this soil, or at least a part of this system . . .

I am going to tell the story—simplified—of certain philosophers. I am going to emphasize only that point of each of their systems which constitutes a slice of *personality* and hence belongs to that incontrovertible, non-debatable evidence which it is the task of history to preserve. It is meant to be a beginning, by means of a comparative approach, toward the recovery and re-creation of certain ancient names, so that the polyphony of Greek nature at long last may resound once more. The task is to bring to light what we *must ever love and honor* and what no subsequent enlightenment can take away: great individual human beings.

A LATER PREFACE

This attempt to tell the story of the older Greek philosophers is distinguished from similar attempts by its brevity. This has been attained by mentioning, for each of the philosophers, but a very small number of doctrines—in other words, by its incompleteness. But I have selected those doctrines which sound most clearly the personality of the individual philosopher, whereas the complete enumeration of all the transmitted doctrines, as it is the custom of the ordinary handbooks to give, has but one sure result: the complete silencing of personality. That is why those reports are so dull. The only thing of interest in a refuted system is the personal element. It alone is what is forever irrefutable. It is possible to present the image of a man in three anecdotes; I shall try to emphasize three anecdotes in each system and abandon the rest.

1

There are people who are opposed to all philosophy and one does well to listen to them, particularly when they advise the diseased minds of Germans to stay away from metaphysics, instead preaching purification through *physis* as Goethe did, or healing through music, as did Richard Wagner. The physicians of our culture repudiate philosophy. Whoever wishes to justify it must show, therefore, to what ends. a healthy culture uses and has used philosophy. Perhaps the sick will then actually gain salutary insight into why philosophy is harmful specifically to them. There are good instances, to be sure, of a type of health which can exist altogether without philosophy, or with but a very moderate, almost playful, exercise of it. The Romans during their best period lived without philosophy. But where could we find an instance of cultural pathology which philosophy restored to health? If philosophy ever manifested itself as helpful, redeeming, or prophylactic, it was in a healthy culture. The sick, it made ever sicker. Wherever a culture was disintegrating, wherever the tension between it and its individual components was slack, philosophy could never re-integrate the individuals back into the group. Wherever an individual was of a mind to stand apart, to draw a circle of self-sufficiency about himself, philosophy was ready to isolate him still further, finally to destroy him through that isolation. Philosophy is dangerous wherever it does not exist in its fullest right, and it is only the health of a culture—and not every culture at that—which accords it such fullest right.

And now let us look around for the highest authority for what we may term cultural health. The Greeks, with their truly healthy culture, have once and for all *justified* philosophy simply by having engaged in it, and engaged in it more fully than any other people. They could not even stop engaging in philosophy at the proper time; even in their skinny old age they retained the hectic postures of ancient suitors, even when all they meant by philosophy was but the pious sophistries and the sacrosanct hair-splittings of Christian dogmatics. By the fact that they were unable to stop in time, they considerably diminished their merit for barbaric posterity, because this posterity, in the ignorance and unrestraint of its youth, was bound to get caught in those too artfully woven nets and ropes.

On the other hand the Greeks knew precisely how to begin at the proper time, and the lesson of how one must start out in philosophy they demonstrate more plainly than any other people. Not to wait until a period of affliction (as those who derive philosophy from personal moroseness imagine), but to begin in the midst of good fortune, at the peak of mature manhood, as a pursuit springing from the ardent joyousness of courageous and victorious maturity. At such a period of their culture the Greeks engaged in philosophy, and this teaches us not only what philosophy is and does, but also gives us information about the Greeks themselves. For if they had been the sober and precocious technicians and the cheerful sensates that the learned philistines of our day imagine they were, or if they had floated solely in a self-indulgent fog, reverberating with heavy breathings and deep feelings, as the unscholarly fantasts among us like to assume, the well-spring of philosophy should never have seen the light of day in Greece. At most it would have produced a rivulet soon to lose itself in the sands or evaporate in a haze. It never could have become that broad proud stream which we know as Greek philosophy.

It has been pointed out assiduously, to be sure, how much the Greeks were able to find and learn abroad in the Orient, and it is doubtless true that they picked up much there. It is a strange spectacle, however, to see the alleged teachers from the Orient and their Greek disciples exhibited side by side: Zoroaster next to Heraclitus, Hindus next to Eleatics, Egyptians next to Empedocles, or even Anaxagoras amidst the Jews and Pythagoras amidst the Chinese. As to specifics, very little has been discovered by such juxtaposition. As to the general idea, we should not mind it, if only its exponents did not burden us with their conclusion that philosophy was thus merely imported into Greece rather than having grown and developed there in a soil natural and native to it. Or worse, that philosophy being alien to the Greeks, it very likely con-

tributed to their ruin more than to their well-
being. Nothing would be sillier than to claim an
autochthonous development for the Greeks. On
the contrary, they invariably absorbed other living cultures. The very reason they got so far is
that they knew how to pick up the spear and
throw it onward from the point where others
had left it. Their skill in the art of fruitful learning was admirable. We ought to be learning
from our neighbors precisely as the Greeks
learned from theirs, not for the sake of learned
pedantry but rather using everything we learn
as a foothold which will take us up as high, and
higher than our neighbor. The quest for philosophy's beginnings is idle, for everywhere in all
beginnings we find only the crude, the unformed,
the empty and the ugly. What matters in all
things is the higher levels. People who prefer to
spend their time on Egyptian or Persian philosophy rather than on Greek, on the grounds that
the former are more "original" and in any event
older, are just as ill-advised as those who cannot
deal with the magnificent, profound mythology
of the Greeks until they have reduced it to the
physical trivialities of sun, lightning, storm and
mist which originally presumably gave rise to
it. They are the people, also, who imagine they
have found a purer form of religion than that of
Greek polytheism when they discover the good
old Aryans restricting their worship to the single
vault of heaven. Everywhere, the way to the beginnings leads to barbarism. Whoever concerns
himself with the Greeks should be ever mindful
that an unrestrained thirst for knowledge for its

own sake barbarizes men just as much as a hatred of knowledge. The Greeks themselves, possessed of an inherently insatiable thirst for knowledge, controlled it by their ideal need for and consideration of all the values of life. Whatever they learned, they wanted to live through, immediately. They engaged in philosophy, as in everything else, as civilized human beings, and with highly civilized aims, wherefore, free of any kind of autochthonous conceit, they forebore trying to re-invent the elements of philosophy and science. Rather they instantly tackled the job of so fulfilling, enhancing, elevating and purifying the elements they took over from elsewhere that they became inventors after all, but in a higher sense and a purer sphere. For what they invented was *the archetypes of philosophic thought.* All posterity has not made an essential contribution to them since.

All other cultures are put to shame by the marvellously idealized philosophical company represented by the ancient Greek masters Thales, Anaximander, Heraclitus, Parmenides, Anaxagoras, Empedocles, Democritus and Socrates. These men are monolithic. Their thinking and their character stand in a relationship characterized by strictest necessity. They are devoid of conventionality, for in their day there was no philosophic or academic professionalism. All of them, in magnificent solitude, were the only ones of their time whose lives were devoted to insight alone. They all possessed that virtuous energy of the ancients, herein excelling all men since, which led them to find their own individual form and to develop it through all its metamorphoses to its subtlest and greatest possibilities. For there was no convention to meet them halfway. Thus all of them together form what Schopenhauer in contrast to the republic of scholars has called the republic of creative minds: each giant calling to his brother through the desolate intervals of time. And undisturbed by the wanton noises of the dwarfs that creep past beneath them, their high spirit-converse continues.

Of this high spirit-converse I have resolved to tell the story. At least whatever part of it our modern hardness of hearing can hear and understand—probably a negligible amount. It seems to me that those ancient wise men, from Thales through Socrates, have touched in their conversation all those things, albeit in their most generalized form, which to our minds constitutes typical Hellenism. In their conversation as in their personalities they form the great-featured mold of Greek genius whose ghostly print, whose blurred and less expressive copy, is the whole of Greek history. If we could interpret correctly the sum total of Greek culture, all we would find would be the reflection of the image which shines forth brightly from its greatest luminaries. The very first experience that philosophy had on Greek soil, the sanction of the Seven Sages, is an unmistakable and unforgettable feature of the Hellenic image. Other peoples have saints; the Greeks have sages. It has been rightly said that a people is characterized not as much by its great men as by the way in which it recognizes and honors its great men. In other times and places, the philosopher is a chance wanderer, lonely in a totally hostile environment which he either creeps past or attacks with clenched fist. Among the Greeks alone, he is not an accident. When he appears in the sixth and fifth centuries, among the enormous dangers and temptations of increasing secularization, walking as it were out of the cave of Trophonius straight into the midst of the lavish luxuriance, the pioneer freedom, the wealth and sensuality of the Greek colonies, we may suspect that he comes, a distinguished warning voice, to express the same purpose to which the tragic drama was born during that century, and of which the Orphic mysteries hint in the grotesque hieroglyphics of their rites. The judgment of those philosophers as to life and existence in general means so much more than any modern judgment, for they had life in lavish perfection before their eyes, whereas the feeling of our thinkers is confused by our split desire for freedom, beauty and greatness on the one hand and our drive toward truth on the other, a drive which asks merely "And what is life worth, after all?" The philosopher's mission when he lives in a genuine culture (which is characterized by unity of style) cannot be properly derived from our own circumstances and experiences, for we have no genuine culture. Only a culture such as the Greeks possessed can answer our question as to the task of the philosopher, and only it, I repeat, can justify philosophy at all, because it alone knows and can demonstrate why and how the philosopher is *not* a chance random wanderer, exiled to this place or to that. There is a steely

necessity which binds a philosopher to a genuine
culture. But what if such a culture does not exist?
Then the philosopher is a comet, incalculable
and therefore terror-inspiring. When all is well,
he shines like a stellar object of the first magnitude in the solar system of culture. That is why
the Greeks justify philosophers. Only among
them, they are not comets.

2

After these reflections I shall presumably be
understood if I speak of the pre-Platonic philosophers as of one homogenous company and plan
to devote this essay to them alone. With Plato,
something entirely new has its beginning. Or it
might be said with equal justice, from Plato on
there is something essentially amiss with philosophers when one compares them to that "republic
of creative minds" from Thales to Socrates.

Whoever wants to point out the disadvan-
tageous aspect of the older masters may call them
one-sided and their posterity, including Plato at
the head, many-sided. But it would be more correct and simple to comprehend the latter as philosophic mixed types, and the former as pure
types. Plato himself is the first mixed type on a
grand scale, expressing his nature in his philosophy no less than in his personality. Socratic,

Pythagorean and Heraclitic elements are all combined in his doctrine of Ideas. This doctrine is not a phenomenon exhibiting a pure philosophic type. As a human being, too, Plato mingles the features of the regal exclusive and self-contained Heraclitus with the melancholy compassionate and legislative Pythagoras and the psychologically acute dialectician Socrates. All subsequent philosophers are such mixed types. Where a certain one-sidedness is paramount in them, in the Cynics for example, it is not a type phenomenon but one of caricature. What is far more important, however, is that the mixed types were founders of sects, and that sectarianism with its institutions and counterinstitutions was opposed to Hellenic culture and its previous unity of style. Such philosophers too sought salvation in their own way, but only for the individual or for a small inside group of friends and disciples. The activity of the older philosophers, on the other hand (though they were quite unconscious of it) tended toward the healing and the purification of the whole. It is the mighty flow of Greek culture that shall not be impeded; the terrible dangers in its path shall be cleared away: thus did the philosopher protect and defend his native land. But later, beginning with Plato, philosophers became exiles, conspiring against their fatherland.

It is a veritable misfortune that we have so little extant of the works of the ancient masters and that not a single one of their works was handed down to us complete. We are involuntarily influenced by this loss, measuring therefore

with false standards, and letting ourselves be disposed more favorably toward Plato and Aristotle
by the sheer accident that they never lacked con-
noisseurs and copyists. Some go so far as to assume a special destiny reserved for books, a *fatum
libellorum*. Such a fate would have to be mali-
cious indeed to deprive us of Heraclitus, of the
wonderful poetry of Empedocles, and of the writ-
ings of Democritus, thought by the ancients to be
Plato's equal and, so far as ingenuity is concerned, his superior, slipping us instead the Stoics, the Epicureans, and Cicero. Very likely the
most impressive part of Greek thought and its
verbal expression is lost to us, a fate not to be
wondered at if one remembers the misfortunes
that befell Scotus Erigena and Pascal and the
fact that in even this enlightened century the
first edition of Schopenhauer's *Welt als Wille
und Vorstellung* had to be sold for wastepaper.
If someone wishes to assume a special fatal power
governing such events, he may do so and say
with Goethe "Do not complain of the mean and
the petty, for regardless of what you have been
told, the mean and the petty are everywhere in
control." That they are more in control than the
power of truth is certainly true. Mankind so
rarely produces a good book, one which with
bold freedom sounds the battle-cry of truth, the
song of philosophic heroism. And yet the most
wretched accidents, sudden eclipses of men's
minds, superstitious paroxysms and antipathies,
cramped or lazy writing fingers, down to book
worms and rainfall, all determine whether or not
a book will live on another century or turn into

ashes and mould. But let us not lament or, in any event, remember the consolatory words with which Hamann put an end to the lamentations of scholars over lost works. "Did not the artist who squeezed a lentil through the eye of a needle find enough lentils in a bushel to practice his acquired skill? One should like to put this question to all the scholars who make no better use of the works of the ancients than that man did of his lentils." In the case before us, we might add, we do not need an additional word, anecdote, or date other than those transmitted to us. In fact we do not need all that we do have, in order to demonstrate our general proposition that the Greeks justify philosophy.

A period which suffers from a so-called high general level of liberal education but which is devoid of culture in the sense of a unity of style which characterizes all its life, will not quite know what to do with philosophy and wouldn't, if the Genius of Truth himself were to proclaim it in the streets and the market places. During such times philosophy remains the learned monologue of the lonely stroller, the accidental loot of the individual, the secret skeleton in the closet, or the harmless chatter between senile academics and children. No one may venture to fulfill philosophy's law with his own person, no one may live philosophically with that simple loyalty which compelled an ancient, no matter where he was or what he was doing, to deport himself as a Stoic if he once had pledged faith to the Stoa. All modern philosophizing is political, policed by governments, churches, academies, custom, fashion, and human cowardice, all of which limit it to a fake learnedness. Our philosophy stops with the sigh "If only . . ." and with the insight "Once upon a time . . ." Philosophy has no rights, and modern man, if he had any courage or conscience, should really repudiate it. He might ban it with words similar to those which Plato used to ban the tragic poets from his state, though reply could be made, just as the tragic poets might have made reply to Plato. If forced for once to speak out, philosophy might readily say, "Wretched people! Is it my fault if I am roaming the country among you like a cheap fortune-teller? If I must hide and disguise myself as though I were a fallen woman and you my judges? Just look at my sister, Art! Like me, she is in exile among barbarians. We no longer know what to do to save ourselves. True, here among you we have lost all our rights, but the judges who shall restore them to us shall judge you too. And to you they shall say: Go get yourselves a culture. Only then you will find out what philosophy can and will do."

3

Greek philosophy seems to begin with an absurd notion, with the proposition that *water* is the primal origin and the womb of all things.

Is it really necessary for us to take serious notice of this proposition? It is, and for three reasons. First, because it tells something about the primal origin of all things; second, because it does so in language devoid of image or fable, and finally, because contained in it, if only embryonically, is the thought, "all things are one." The first reason still leaves Thales in the company of the religious and the superstitious; the second takes him out of such company and shows him as a natural scientist, but the third makes him the first Greek philosopher. Had he said, "water turns into earth," we should have but a scientific hypothesis, a wrong one but difficult to disprove. But he went beyond scientific considerations. By presenting his unity-concept in the form of his water-hypothesis, Thales did not, it is true, overcome the low level of empiric insight prevalent in his time. What he did was to pass over its horizon. The sparse and un-ordered observations of an empirical nature which he made regarding the occurrence and the transformations of water (more specifically, of moisture) would have allowed, much less made advisable, no such gigantic generalization. What drove him to it was a metaphysical conviction which had its origin in a mystic intuition. We meet it in every philosophy, together with the ever-renewed attempts at a more suitable expression, this proposition that "all things are one."

It is strange how high-handedly such a faith deals with all empiricism. In connection with Thales, particularly, we can learn what philosophy has always done when it would reach its magnetically attractive goal past all the hedges of experience. Philosophy leaps ahead on tiny toe-holds; hope and intuition lend wings to its feet. Calculating reason lumbers heavily behind, looking for better footholds, for reason too wants to reach that alluring goal which its divine com-rade has long since reached. It is like seeing two mountain climbers standing before a wild mountain stream that is tossing boulders along its course: one of them light-footedly leaps over it, using the rocks to cross, even though behind and beneath him they hurtle into the depths. The other stands helpless; he must first build himself a fundament which will carry his heavy cautious steps. Occasionally this is not possible, and then there exists no god who can help him across. What then is it that brings philosophical thinking so quickly to its goal? Is it different from the thinking that calculates and measures, only by virtue of the greater rapidity with which it transcends all space? No, its feet are propelled by an alien, illogical power—the power of crea-tive imagination. Lifted by it, it leaps from pos-sibility to possibility, using each one as a tem-porary resting place. Occasionally it will grasp such a resting place even as it flies. Creative premonition will show the place; imagination guesses from afar that here it will find a demon-strable resting place. But the special strength of imagination is its lightning-quick seizure and illumination of analogies. Subsequent reflection comes with measuring devices and routinizing patterns and tries to replace analogy with equa-tion and synchronicity with causality. But even if

this should not work, even in a case such as that
of Thales, non-provable philosophic thinking
has its value. Even if all the footholds have
crumbled by the time logic and empiric rigidity
want to cross over to such a proposition as "all
is water," even after the total demolition of any
scientific edifice, something remains. And in this
remainder lies an impelling force which is the
hope of future fruitfulness.

I do not mean, of course, that Thales' thought
in some attenuated or restricted sense contains
a sort of poetic truth. One might imagine there
could be some sort of value in it for an artist,
for example, who while standing by a waterfall
and seeing in the watery masses that leap toward him the playfully created models of men,
animals, masks, plants, rocks, nymphs, griffins—
the whole typology, in fact, of sculpture—might
well find the proposition, "all is water," a true
one. On the contrary, the thought of Thales—
even after the realization that it is unprovable—
has its value precisely in the fact that it was
meant non-mythically and non-allegorically. The
Greeks, among whom Thales stood out so suddenly, were the very opposite of realists, in that
they believed only in the reality of men and gods,
looking upon all of nature as but a disguise, a
masquerade, or a metamorphosis of these god-
men. Man for them was the truth and the core of
all things; everything else was but semblance and
the play of illusion. For this very reason they
found it unbelievably difficult to comprehend
concepts as such. Herein they were the exact opposite of modern man. For us, even the most per-

sonal is sublimated back into an abstraction; for
them, the greatest abstraction kept running back
into a person. But Thales said, "Not man, but
water is the reality of all things." He begins to
believe in nature, by believing at least in water.
Being a mathematician and astronomer, he had
turned cold against everything mythical and allegorical, and if he did not become quite sober
enough to reach the pure abstraction "all things
are one," instead remaining at a concrete expression of it, he was nonetheless an alien rarity
among the Greeks of his time. The highly con-
spicuous Orphics perhaps had the capacity of
comprehending and thinking abstractions without concrete aids to an even greater degree than
Thales did. But they succeeded in expressing it
only in allegorical form. Pherecydes of Syros, too,
who is chronologically and in several empirical
concepts close to Thales, hovers with his utterances in that middle region in which mythology
and allegory are wedded. He dares, for example,
to compare the earth with a winged oak which
hangs high in the air with wide-spread pinions
and which Zeus, after his conquest of Chronos,
covers with the magnificent robe of honor on
which he himself has embroidered all the lands
and waters and rivers of earth. Compared with
such obscure allegorical philosophizing, barely
translatable into the realm of visibility, Thales
is a creative master who began to see into the
depths of nature without the help of fantastic
fable. If in so doing he used and then passed
over the methods of science and of proof he but
demonstrates a typical characteristic of the phil-

osophic mind. The Greek word designating "sage" is etymologically related to *sapio*, I taste, *sapiens*, he who tastes, *sisyphos*, the man of keenest taste. A sharp savoring and selecting, a meaningful discriminating, in other words, makes out the peculiar art of the philosopher, in the eyes of the people. The philosopher is not a man of intellect, if by stressing intellect one designates a person who can see to the success of his personal undertakings. Aristotle rightly says that "What Thales and Anaxagoras know will be considered unusual, astonishing, difficult and divine, but never useful, for their concern was not with the good of humanity." Philosophy is distinguished from science by its selectivity and its discrimination of the unusual, the astonishing, the difficult and the divine, just as it is distinguished from intellectual cleverness by its emphasis on the useless. Science rushes headlong, without selectivity, without "taste," at whatever is knowable, in the blind desire to know all at any cost. Philosophical thinking, on the other hand, is ever on the scent of those things which are most worth knowing, the great and the important insights. Now the concept of greatness is changeable, in the realm of morality as well as in that of esthetics. And so philosophy starts by legislating greatness. Part of this is a sort of name-giving. "This is a great thing," says philosophy, thereby elevating man over the blind unrestrained greed of his drive for knowledge. By its concept of greatness philosophy tames this drive, and most of all considering the greatest knowledge of all, the knowledge of the essence and

core of all things, as ascertainable and, in fact, as-
certained. When Thales says, "all is water," man
is stung up out of the wormlike probings and
creepings-about of his separate sciences. He in-
tuits the ultimate resolution of all things and
overcomes, by means of such intuition, the vulgar restrictions of the lower levels of knowledge.
The philosopher seeks to hear within himself the
echoes of the world symphony and to re-project
them in the form of concepts. While he is con-
templative-perceptive like the artist, compassionate like the religious, a seeker of purposes and
causalities like the scientist, even while he feels
himself swelling into a macrocosm, he all the
while retains a certain self-possession, a way of
viewing himself coldly as a mirror of the world.
This is the same sense of self-possession which
characterizes the dramatic artist who transforms
himself into alien bodies and talks with their alien
tongues and yet can project this transformation
into written verse that exists in the outside world
on its own. What verse is for the poet, dialectical
thinking is for the philosopher. He grasps for it
in order to get hold of his own enchantment, in
order to perpetuate it. And just as for the drama-
tist words and verse are but the stammering of an
alien tongue, needed to tell what he has seen
and lived, what he could utter directly only
through music or gesture, just so every profound
philosophic intuition expressed through dialectic and through scientific reflection is the only
means for the philosopher to communicate what
he has seen. But it is a sad means; basically a

metaphoric and entirely unfaithful translation
into a totally different sphere and speech. Thus
Thales had seen the unity of all that is, but
when he went to communicate it, he found himself talking about water!

4

While the archetype of the philosopher
emerges with the image of Thales only as out of
shifting mists, the image of his great successor
already speaks much more plainly to us. Anaximander of Miletus, the first philosophical author
of the ancients, writes exactly as one expects a
typical philosopher to write when alienating demands have not yet robbed him of his innocence
and naiveté. That is to say, in graven stylized
letters, sentence after sentence the witness to
fresh illumination, each the expression of time
spent in sublime meditation. Each single thought
and its form is a milestone upon the path to the
highest wisdom. Thus, with lapidary impressive-
ness, Anaximander says upon one occasion,
"Where the source of things is, to that place they
must also pass away, according to necessity, for
they must pay penance and be judged for their
injustices, in accordance with the ordinance of
time." Enigmatic proclamation of a true pes-

simist, oracular legend over the boundary stone
of Greek philosophy: how shall we interpret
you?

The only serious moralist of our century in
Parergis (Vol. II, Chapter 12) charges us with a
similar reflection. "The proper measure with
which to judge any and all human beings is that
they are really creatures who should not exist
at all and who are doing penance for their lives
by their manifold sufferings and their death.
What could we expect of such creatures? Are we
not all sinners under sentence of death? We do
penance for having been born, first by living and
then by dying." A man who can read such a lesson in the physiognomy of our common human
lot, who can recognize the basic poor quality of
any and all human life in the very fact that
not one of us will bear close scrutiny (although
our era, infected with the biographical plague,
seems to think quite different and statelier
thoughts as to the dignity of man), a man who,
like Schopenhauer, has heard "upon the heights
of India's clear air" the holy word of the moral
value of existence—such a man will find it difficult to keep from indulging in a highly anthropomorphic metaphor. He will extract that
melancholy doctrine from its application to human life and project it unto the general quality
of all existence. It may not be logical, but it certainly is human, to view now, together with Anaximander, all coming-to-be as though it were an
illegitimate emancipation from eternal being, a
wrong for which destruction is the only penance.
Everything that has ever come-to-be again passes

away, whether we think of human life or of water or of hot and cold. Wherever definite qualities are perceivable, we can prophesy, upon the basis of enormously extensive experience, the passing away of these qualities. Never, in other words, can a being which possesses definite qualities or consists of such be the origin or first principle of things. That which truly *is*, concludes Anaximander, cannot possess definite characteristics, or it would come-to-be and pass away like all the other things. In order that coming-to-be shall not cease, primal being must be indefinite. The immortality and everlastingness of primal being does not lie in its infinitude or its inexhaustibility, as the commentators of Anaximander generally assume, but in the fact that it is devoid of definite qualities that would lead to its passing. Hence its name, "the indefinite." Thus named, the primal being is superior to that which comes to be, insuring thereby eternity and the unimpeded course of coming-to-be. This ultimate unity of the "indefinite," the womb of all things, can, it is true, be designated by human speech only as a negative, as something to which the existent world of coming-to-be can give no predicate. We may look upon it as the equal of the Kantian *Ding an sich*.

Now anyone who can quarrel as to what sort of primal stuff this could have been, whether an intermediate substance between air and water or perhaps between air and fire, has certainly not understood our philosopher at all. This is equally true of those who ask themselves seriously whether Anaximander thought of his primal substance as perhaps a mixture of all existent materials. Instead, we must direct our glance to that lapidary sentence which we cited earlier, to the place where we may learn that Anaximander was no longer dealing with the question of the origin of this world in a purely physical way. Rather, when he saw in the multiplicity of things that have come-to-be a sum of injustices that must be expiated, he grasped with bold fingers the tangle of the profoundest problem in ethics. He was the first Greek to do so. How can anything pass away which has a right to be? Whence that restless, ceaseless coming-into-being and giving birth, whence that grimace of painful disfiguration on the countenance of nature, whence the never-ending dirge in all the realms of existence? From this world of injustice, of insolent apostasy from the primeval one-ness of all things, Anaximander flees into a metaphysical fortress from which he leans out, letting his gaze sweep the horizon. At last, after long pensive silence, he puts a question to all creatures: "What is your existence worth? And if it is worthless, why are you here? Your guilt, I see, causes you to tarry in your existence. With your death, you have to expiate it. Look how your earth is withering, how your seas are diminishing and drying up; the seashell on the mountain top can show you how much has dried up already. Even now, fire is destroying your world; some day it will go up in fumes and smoke. But ever and anew, another such world of ephemerality will construct itself. Who is there that could redeem you from the curse of coming-to-be?"

A man who poses questions such as these, whose thinking in its upward flight kept breaking all empirical ropes, catching, instead, at superlunary ones—such a man very likely does not welcome an ordinary mode of living. We can easily credit the tradition that he walked the earth clad in an especially dignified garment and displayed a truly tragic pride in his gestures and customs of daily living. He lived as he wrote; he spoke as solemnly as he dressed; he lifted his hands and placed his feet as though this existence were a tragic drama into which he had been born to play a hero. In all these things, he was the great model for Empedocles. His fellow-citizens elected him to lead a colony of emigrants. Perhaps they were glad to honor him and get rid of him at the same time. His thought, too, emigrated and founded colonies. In Ephesus and in Elea, people could not rid themselves of it, and if they could not make up their minds to remain where it left them, they also knew that they had been led there by it, and that it was from there they would travel on without it.

Thales demonstrated the need to simplify the realm of the many, to reduce it to the mere unfolding or masking of the *one* and only existent quality, water. Anaximander takes two steps beyond him. For the first, he asks himself: How is the many possible if there is such a thing as the eternal one? And he takes his answer from the self-contradictory, self-consuming and negating character of the many. Its existence becomes for him a moral phenomenon. It is not justified, but expiates itself forever through its passing.

But then he sees another question: Why hasn't all that came-to-be passed away long since, since a whole eternity of time has passed? Whence the ever-renewed stream of coming-to-be? And from this question he can save himself only by a mystic possibility: eternal coming-to-be can have its origin only in eternal being; the conditions for the fall from being to coming-to-be in injustice are forever the same; the constellation of things is such that no end can be envisaged for the emergence of individual creatures from the womb of the "indefinite." Here Anaximander stopped, which means he remained in the deep shadows which lie like gigantic ghosts upon the mountains of this world view. The closer men wanted to get to the problem of how the definite could ever fall from the indefinite, the ephemeral from the eternal, the unjust from the just, the deeper grew the night.

5

Straight at that mystic night in which was shrouded Anaximander's problem of becoming, walked *Heraclitus* of Ephesus and illuminated it by a divine stroke of lightning. " 'Becoming' is what I contemplate," he exclaims, "and no one else has watched so attentively this everlasting wavebeat and rhythm of things. And what did I see? Lawful order, unfailing certainties, ever-like orbits of lawfulness, *Erinnyes* sitting in judgment on all transgressions against lawful order, the whole world the spectacle of sovereign justice and of the demonically ever-present natural forces that serve it. Not the punishment of what has come-to-be did I see, but the justification of that which is coming-into-being. When did hybris, when did apostasy ever reveal itself in inviolable forms, in laws held sacred? Where injustice rules, there are caprice, disorder, lawlessness, contradiction. But where law and Zeuz's daughter *Dike* rule alone, as they do in this world, how could there be the sphere of guilt, of penance, of judgment? How could this world be the execution-arena of all that is condemned?"

From such intuition Heraclitus derived two connected negations. Only through comparison with the doctrines of his predecessor can they be illuminated. One, he denied the duality of totally diverse worlds—a position which Anaximander had been compelled to assume. He no longer distinguished a physical world from a metaphysical one, a realm of definite qualities from an undefinable "indefinite." And after this first step, nothing could hold him back from a second, far bolder negation: he altogether denied being. For this one world which he retained—supported by eternal unwritten laws, flowing upward and downward in brazen rhythmic beat—nowhere shows a tarrying, an indestructibility, a bulwark in the stream. Louder than Anaximander, Heraclitus proclaimed: "I see nothing other than becoming. Be not deceived. It is the fault

of your myopia, not of the nature of things, if
you believe you see land somewhere in the ocean
of coming-to-be and passing away. You use names
for things as though they rigidly, persistently en-
dured; yet even the stream into which you step
a second time is not the one you stepped into
before."

Heraclitus' regal possession is his extraordinary power to think intuitively. Toward the
other type of thinking, the type that is accomplished in concepts and logical combinations, in
other words toward reason, he shows himself
cool, insensitive, in fact hostile, and seems to feel
pleasure whenever he can contradict it with an
intuitively arrived-at truth. He does this in dicta
like "Everything forever has its opposite along
with it," and in such unabashed fashion that
Aristotle accused him of the highest crime before
the tribunal of reason: to have sinned against
the law of contradiction. But intuitive thinking
embraces two things: one, the present many-col-
ored and changing world that crowds in upon
us in all our experiences, and two, the conditions
which alone make any experience of this world
possible: time and space. For they may be per-
ceived intuitively, even without a definite content, independent of all experience, purely in
themselves. Now when Heraclitus contemplates
time in this fashion, apart from all experience,
he finds in it the most instructive monogram of
everything that might conceivably come under
the head of intuition. As Heraclitus sees time, so
does Schopenhauer. He repeatedly said of it that
every moment in it exists only insofar as it has

just consumed the preceding one, its father, and is then immediately consumed likewise. And that past and future are as perishable as any dream, but that the present is but the dimensionless and durationless borderline between the two. And that space is just like time, and that everything which coexists in space and time has but a relative existence, that each thing exists through and for another like it, which is to say through and for an equally relative one.—This is a truth of the greatest immediate self-evidence for everyone, and one which for this very reason is extremely difficult to reach by way of concept or reason. But whoever finds himself directly looking at it must at once move on to the Heraclitan conclusion and say that the whole nature of reality [*Wirklichkeit*] lies simply in its acts [*Wirken*] and that for it there exists no other sort of being. Schopenhauer elucidates this point also (*Welt als Wille und Vorstellung*, Vol. I, Book 1, § 4):

> Only by way of its acts does [reality] fill space and time. Its activity upon the immediate object conditions the intuitive perception in which alone it has existence. The consequence of the activity of any material object upon another is recognized only insofar as the latter now acts differently from what it did before upon the immediate object. Reality consists of nothing other than this. Cause and effect [*Wirkung*] in other words make out the whole nature of materiality: its being is its activity. That is why in German the epitome of all materiality is properly called *Wirklichkeit* [actu-

ality], a word much more apt than *Realität.*
That upon which it acts is likewise invariably
matter; its whole being and nature consists
only in the orderly changes which one of its
parts produces in another. *Wirklichkeit* therefore is completely relative, in accordance with
a relationship that is valid only within its
bounds, exactly as is time, exactly as is space.

The everlasting and exclusive coming-to-be,
the impermanence of everything actual, which
constantly acts and comes-to-be but never is, as
Heraclitus teaches it, is a terrible, paralyzing
thought. Its impact on men can most nearly be
likened to the sensation during an earthquake
when one loses one's familiar confidence in a
firmly grounded earth. It takes astonishing
strength to transform this reaction into its opposite, into sublimity and the feeling of blessed
astonishment. Heraclitus achieved this by means
of an observation regarding the actual process
of all coming-to-be and passing away. He con-
ceived it under the form of polarity, as being
the diverging of a force into two qualitatively
different opposed activities that seek to re-unite.
Everlastingly, a given quality contends against
itself and separates into opposites; everlastingly
these opposites seek to re-unite. Ordinary people
fancy they see something rigid, complete and
permanent; in truth, however, light and dark,
bitter and sweet are attached to each other and
interlocked at any given moment like wrestlers
of whom sometimes the one, sometimes the other
is on top. Honey, says Heraclitus, is at the same
time bitter and sweet; the world itself is a mixed

drink which must constantly be stirred. The strife of the opposites gives birth to all that comes-to-be; the definite qualities which look permanent to us express but the momentary ascendency of one partner. But this by no means signifies the end of the war; the contest endures in all eternity. Everything that happens, happens in accordance with this strife, and it is just in the strife that eternal justice is revealed. It is a wonderful idea, welling up from the purest strings of Hellenism, the idea that strife embodies the everlasting sovereignty of strict justice, bound to everlasting laws. Only a Greek was capable of finding such an idea to be the fundament of a cosmology; it is Hesiod's good *Eris* transformed into the cosmic principle; it is the contest-idea of the Greek individual and the Greek state, taken from the gymnasium and the palaestra, from the artist's *agon,* from the contest between political parties and between cities—all transformed into universal application so that now the wheels of the cosmos turn on it. Just as the Greek individual fought as though he alone were right and an infinitely sure measure of judicial opinion were determining the trend of victory at any given moment, so the qualities wrestle with one another, in accordance with inviolable laws and standards that are immanent in the struggle. The things in whose definiteness and endurance narrow human minds, like animal minds, believe have no real existence. They are but the flash and spark of drawn swords, the quick radiance of victory in the struggle of the opposites.

That struggle which is peculiar to all coming-to-be, that everlasting alternation of victory, is again something also described by Schopenhauer *Welt als Wille und Vorstellung*, Vol. I, Book 2, § 27):

> Forever and ever, persistent matter must change its form. Grasping the clue of causality, mechanical, physical, chemical and organic phenomena greedily push to the fore, snatching matter from one another, for each would reveal its own inherent idea. We can follow this strife throughout the whole of nature. In fact we might say that nature exists but by virtue of it.

The pages that follow this passage give some notable illustrations of such struggle, except that the basic tone of their description is quite different from that which Heraclitus offers, because strife for Schopenhauer is a proof of the internal self-dissociation of the Will to Live, which is seen as a self-consuming, menacing and gloomy drive, a thoroughly frightful and by no means blessed phenomenon. The arena and the object of the struggle is matter, which the natural forces alternately try to snatch from one another, as well as space and time whose union by means of causality is this very matter.

6

While Heraclitus' imagination was eyeing this never-ceasing motion of the cosmos, this "actuality," like a blissful spectator who is watching innumerable pairs of contestants wrestling in joyous combat and refereed by stern judges, a still greater intuition overtook him. He could no longer see the contesting pairs and their referees as separate; the judges themselves seemed to be striving in the contest and the contestants seemed to be judging them. Now, perceiving basically nothing but everlastingly sovereign justice itself, he dared proclaim: "The struggle of the many is pure justice itself! In fact, the one is the many. For what are all those qualities, in essence? Are they the immortal gods? Are they separate beings, acting on and in themselves, from the beginning and without end? And if the world which we see knows only coming-to-be and passing away, but no tarrying, is it possible that those qualities might constitute a different kind of world, a metaphysical one? Not a world of unity, to be sure, such as Anaximander sought beyond the fluttering veils of the many, but a world of eternal substantive multiplicities?" Did Heraclitus take a detour, after all, back into a dual world order, however violently he might deny it,

with an Olympus of numerous immortal gods
and demons—of *many* realities in other words—
and with a human world which sees but the dust
cloud of the Olympic battle and the flash of divine spears—a coming-into-being, in other words?
Anaximander had fled into the womb of the
metaphysical "indefinite" to escape the definite
qualities; because they came-to-be and passed
away, he had denied them true, nuclear existence. But does it now look as though "becoming"
were but the coming-to-be-visible of the struggle
between eternal qualities? Should our talk of
coming-to-be perhaps be derived from the peculiar weakness of human insight, whereas in the
true nature of things there is no coming-to-be
at all, but only a synchronicity of many true
realities which were not born and will not die?

But these are un-Heraclitan loop-holes and
labyrinths. Once again he proclaims, "The one is
the many." The many perceivable qualities are
neither eternal substances nor fantasms of our
senses (Anaxagoras is later to imagine the
former, Parmenides the latter); they are neither
rigid autocratic being nor fleeting semblance
flitting through human minds. The third possibility, the only one for Heraclitus, cannot be
guessed by dialectic detective work nor figured
out with the help of calculations. For what he
here invented is a rarity even in the sphere of
mystic incredibilities and unexpected cosmic
metaphors. "The world is the *game* Zeus plays,"
or, expressed more concretely, "of the fire with
itself. This is the only sense in which the one
is at the same time the many."

In order to elucidate the introduction of fire as a cosmos-creating force, I remind the reader of the way in which Anaximander had developed the theory of water as the primal origin of things. Essentially trusting Thales, and supporting his observations with new evidence, Anaximander yet could not convince himself that there was no further quality-stage before water—beyond water as it were. It seemed to him as though the moist formed itself from warm and cold, and warm and cold, therefore, seemed to be preliminary stages of water, the even more aboriginal qualities. With their departure from the primal essence of the "indefinite," coming-to-be begins. Heraclitus who, as far as being a physicist was concerned, subordinated himself to Anaximander, re-interprets the Anaximandrian warm as warm breath, dry vapor, in other words, as fire. Of this fire he now says what Thales and Anaximander had said of water; that it coursed in countless transformations through the orbits of becoming; above all, in its three major occurrences as warmth, moisture and solidity. For water is transformed into earth on its way down, into fire on its way up, or, as Heraclitus seems to have declared more precisely: from the sea rise only the pure vapors which nourish the heavenly fire of the celestial bodies; from the earth only the dark misty ones, from which moisture draws its nourishment. The pure vapors are the transformation of sea into fire, the impure ones the transformation of earth to water. Thus the two transformation-orbits of fire run forever upward and downward, back and forth,

side by side: from fire to water, from thence to
earth, from earth back to water, from water to
fire. While Heraclitus is Anaximander's disciple
as to the main ideas, such as fire being fed by
vapors, or water separating into earth and fire,
he is independent of Anaximander and in opposition to him in that he excludes cold from the
physical process. Anaximander had juxtaposed
cold and warm as equal terms, in order to produce moisture from both. Heraclitus of necessity
could not allow this, for if everything is fire, then
in spite of all its transformations there can be
no such thing as an absolute opposite. Hence he
probably interpreted what is called "cold" as
but a degree of warmth. He certainly could have
justified such an interpretation without any dif-
ficulty. But far more important than this devia-
tion from Anaximander's doctrine is a further
agreement. He believes, like Anaximander, in a
periodically repeated end of the world, and in
an ever renewed rise of another world out of
the all-destroying cosmic fire. The period in
which the world hurries toward the conflagration
and dissolves into pure fire Heraclitus characterizes, with notable emphasis, as a desire, a want,
or lack; the full consumption in fire he calls
satiety. It remains for us to ask how he interpreted and what he might have called the newly
awakening impulse toward cosmic formation, the
new outpouring into the forms of plurality. The
Greek proverb "Satiety gives birth to hybris"
seems to come to our aid here, and indeed one
may ask, for a moment, if Heraclitus did not perhaps derive the return to the many from hybris.

We have but to take this thought seriously to see by its illumination how the countenance of Heraclitus is transformed before our eyes. The proud light in his eyes is extinguished, wrinkles of painful renunciation, of impotence, become apparent; we seem to know why later antiquity called him the "weeping philosopher." Is not the entire world process now an act of punishment for hybris? The many the result of evil-doing? The transformation of the pure into the impure the consequence of injustice? Is guilt not now transplanted into the very nucleus of materiality and the world of becoming and of individuals thereby unburdened of responsibility, to be sure, but simultaneously sentenced to carry the consequences of evil forever and anew?

7

That dangerous word hybris is indeed the touchstone for every Heraclitan. Here he must show whether he has understood or failed to recognize his master. Do guilt, injustice, contradiction and suffering exist in this world?

They do, proclaims Heraclitus, but only for the limited human mind which sees things apart but not connected, not for the con-tuitive god. For him all contradictions run into harmony, invisible to the common human eye, yet under-

standable to one who, like Heraclitus, is related
to the contemplative god. Before his fire-gaze not
a drop of injustice remains in the world poured
all around him; even that cardinal impulse that
allows pure fire to inhabit such impure forms
is mastered by him with a sublime metaphor. In
this world only play, play as artists and children
engage in it, exhibits coming-to-be and passing
away, structuring and destroying, without any
moral additive, in forever equal innocence. And
as children and artists play, so plays the ever-liv-
ing fire. It constructs and destroys, all in innocence. Such is the game that the aeon plays
with itself. Transforming itself into water and
earth, it builds towers of sand like a child at
the seashore, piles them up and tramples them
down. From time to time it starts the game anew.
An instant of satiety—and again it is seized by its
need, as the artist is seized by his need to create.
Not hybris but the ever self-renewing impulse
to play calls new worlds into being. The child
throws its toys away from time to time—and
starts again, in innocent caprice. But when it
does build, it combines and joins and forms its
structures regularly, conforming to inner laws.

Only aesthetic man can look thus at the world,
a man who has experienced in artists and in the
birth of art objects how the struggle of the many
can yet carry rules and laws inherent in itself,
how the artist stands contemplatively above and
at the same time actively within his work, how
necessity and random play, oppositional tension
and harmony, must pair to create a work of art.

Who could possibly demand from such a phi-

losophy an ethic with its necessary imperatives
"thou shalt," or, worse yet, accuse Heraclitus
of lacking such! Man is necessity down to his
last fibre, and totally "unfree," that is if one
means by freedom the foolish demand to be able
to change one's *essentia* arbitrarily, like a garment—a demand which every serious philosophy
has rejected with the proper scorn. Very few
people live consciously by the standards of the
logos and the all-encompassing eye of the artist,
and their eyes and ears and their intellect in
general is a poor witness when "moist slime
fills their souls." Why this is, is not asked, just
as it is not asked why fire turns into water and
earth. Heraclitus after all had no reason why
he *had* to prove (as Leibnitz did) that this is
the best of all possible worlds. It is enough
for him that it is the beautiful innocent game of
the aeon. Man, generally speaking, is for Heraclitus an irrational creature which is no contradiction of the fact that in all aspects of his nature
the law of sovereign reason is fulfilled. He does
not occupy an especially favored position in nature, whose loftiest phenomenon is fire, as ex-
emplified by the celestial bodies. By no means
is simple-minded man an equally lofty phenomenon. Insofar as he shares, of necessity, in fire, he
has a plus of rationality; insofar as he consists
of water and earth, his reason is in a bad way.
There is no obligation on man to recognize the
logos just because he is man. But why does
water, why does earth exist? This, for Heraclitus, is a much more serious question than why
human beings are so stupid and so wicked. The

same immanent lawful order and justice reveals
itself in the highest and in the wrongest man.
But if we press upon Heraclitus the question
why fire is not always fire, why it is sometimes
water and sometimes earth, he could only say,
"It is a game. Don't take it so pathetically and
—above all—don't make morality of it!" Heraclitus only describes the world as it is and takes
the same contemplative pleasure in it that an
artist does when he looks at his own work in
progress. Gloomy, melancholy, tearful, sinister,
bilious, pessimistic, generally hateful: only those
can find him thus who have good cause to be
dissatisfied with his natural history of mankind.
But he would consider such people negligible,
together with their antipathies and sympathies,
their hatreds and their loves, and only conde-
scend to offer advice like "Dogs bark at everyone
whom they do not recognize," or "Donkeys prefer
straw to gold."

Such dissatisfied people are also responsible for
the numerous complaints about the obscurity of
Heraclitus' style. The fact is that hardly anyone
has ever written with as lucid and luminous a
quality. Very tersely, to be sure, and for that
reason obscure for readers who skim and race.
How can people imagine that a philosopher
would intentionally write obscurely—as they
often say of Heraclitus—barring that he has
good cause for hiding certain thoughts, or else
were rascal enough to hide his thought-lessness
behind words. After all, even in matters of ordinary practical life one must, as Schopenhauer
says, be most careful to make one's meaning

plain in order to prevent misunderstanding, if possible; how could one then permit oneself to express unclearly or enigmatically those most difficult, abstruse, scarcely attainable goals of thinking that it is philosophy's task to express. So far as terseness is concerned, however, Jean Paul has a useful admonition:

> Generally speaking, it is quite right if great things—things of much sense for men of rare sense—are expressed but briefly and (hence) darkly, so that barren minds will declare it to be nonsense, rather than translate it into a nonsense that they can comprehend. For mean, vulgar minds have an ugly facility for seeing in the profoundest and most pregnant utterance only their own everyday opinion.

Nonetheless Heraclitus has not escaped the "barren minds"; already the Stoics re-interpreted him on a shallow level, dragging down his basically esthetic perception of cosmic play to signify a vulgar consideration for the world's useful ends, especially those which benefit the human race. His physics became, in their hands, a crude optimism with the continual invitation to Tom, Dick and Harry to *plaudite amici*.

8

Heraclitus was proud, and when a philosopher exhibits pride, it is a great pride indeed. His

activities never directed him toward any "public," toward any applause from the masses or toward the encouraging chorus of his contemporaries. To walk alone along a lonely street is part
of the philosopher's nature. His gift is the rarest
gift of all, the most unnatural one in a certain
sense, exclusive and hostile even toward others
with similar gifts. The wall of his self-sufficiency
must be built of diamonds if it is not to be des-
troyed and broken into, for everything and everyone is in league against him. His journey toward immortality is more difficult and burden-
some than that of other men. And yet no one
can believe more firmly than the philosopher
that his journeying will lead to the goal, for
where could he stand but on the wide-spread
pinions of all time. A lack of consideration for
what is here and now lies at the very core of the
great philosophical nature. He has hold of
truth: let the wheel of time roll where it will,
it can never escape truth. It is important to find
out from such people that they once existed.
Never, for example, could one imagine such pride
as that of Heraclitus, simply as an idle possibility.
Looked at from a general point of view, all striving for insight seems, by its very nature, forever
dissatisfied and unsatisfactory. No one will believe, therefore, in such regal self-esteem and
calm conviction that he is the only rewarded
wooer of truth, except by the instruction of history that such a man did once exist. Such men
live inside their own solar system; only there
can we look for them. A Pythagoras, an Empedocles too, treated himself with an almost

super-human esteem, almost with religious reverence, but the great conviction of metempsychosis and of the unity of all life led him back to other human beings, for their salvation and redemption. The feeling of solitude, however, that pierced the Ephesian hermit of the temple of Artemis, we can intuit only when we are freezing on wild desolate mountains of our own. No all-powerful feeling of compassionate emotions, no desire to help, to heal, to save, stream forth from Heraclitus. He is a star devoid of atmosphere. His eye, flaming toward its inward center, looks outward dead and icy, with but the semblance of sight. All around him, to the very edge of the fortress of his pride beat the waves of illusion and of wrong-ness. Nauseated, he turns from them. But other men, too, those with feeling hearts, turn away in turn from such a mask, cast as it were in brass. Perhaps in some remote sanctum, among idols, surrounded by a cold serene sublime architecture, such a creature may seem more comprehensible. Among human beings, Heraclitus as a human being was unbelievable. Even if he were seen observing the games of noisy children, what he was thinking was surely what no other man had thought on such an occasion. He was thinking of the game of the great world-child Zeus. He did not need human beings, not even those who would benefit from his insights. Whatever one might ask of him, and what the other sages did seek to ask of him, did not interest him. He spoke deprecatingly of such questing, fact-gathering, "historical" men. "I sought and consulted myself," he said, using a word which is used to signify the consultation of an oracle, just as though he and none other were the true fulfiller and perfector of the Delphic dictum, "Know thyself."

But what he heard as he listened to this oracle, he took for immortal wisdom, forever to be reinterpreted, of unlimited effectiveness upon far distant times. The model was the prophetic speeches of the Sibyl. There is enough to last humanity into the farthest future, even if they only interpreted him as though he were verily the oracle and spoke, like the Delphic god, "neither expressing nor hiding." And though the oracle is announced by him "without smile, ornamentation or incense" but with "foaming mouth," it *must* penetrate to the many thousands of years of the future. For the world forever needs the truth, hence the world forever needs Heraclitus, though Heraclitus does not need the world. What care he for fame! Fame among "forever flowing mortals" as he exclaims scornfully. His fame concerns humanity, not him; the immortality of humanity needs him, not he the immortality of the man Heraclitus. What he saw, the teaching of *law in becoming* and of *play in necessity,* must be seen from now on in all eternity. He raised the curtain on this greatest of all dramas.

9

While each word of Heraclitus expresses the pride and the majesty of truth, but of truth grasped in intuitions rather than attained by the rope ladder of logic, while in Sibylline rapture Heraclitus gazes but does not peer, knows but does not calculate, his contemporary Parmenides stands beside him as counter-image, likewise expressing a type of truth-teller but one formed of ice rather than fire, pouring cold piercing light all around.

Once in his life Parmenides, probably at a fairly advanced age, had a moment of purest absolutely bloodless abstraction, unclouded by any reality. This moment—un-Greek as no other in the two centuries of the Tragic Age—whose product is the doctrine of Being—became for Parmenides' own life the boundary stone that separates two periods. At the same time however, this moment divides pre-Socratic thinking into two halves. The first might be called the Anaximandrian period, the second the Parmenidean proper. The first, older period of Parmenides' own philosophizing still bears Anaximandrian traces; it brought forth an organized philosophic-physical system in answer to Anaximander's questions. When later Parmenides was seized by that

icy tremor of abstraction and came face to face
with his utterly simple proposition as to being
and nonbeing, his own previous teachings joined
the rubbish-heap of the older doctrines. Still, he
seems not to have lost every trace of paternal
good-will toward the sturdy and well-made child
of his youth, and he helped himself out by say-
ing, "There is only one right way, to be sure,
but if one wishes for a change to try another,
then my former view, as to quality and consistency, is the only right one." Guarding himself
by this approach, he awarded to his former physical system a dignified and extensive position,
even in that great poem on nature which was
meant to proclaim his new insight as really the
only way of truth. This paternal solicitude, even
considering that it might have crept in by error,
presents the only trace of human sentiment in a
nature wholly petrified by logical rigidity and almost transformed into a thinking machine.

Parmenides, whose personal acquaintance with
Anaximander does not seem unbelievable to me,
and whose starting position from Anaximander's
doctrines is not merely credible but evident, had
the same distrust toward a total separation of
a world which only is and a world which only
comes-to-be that Heraclitus too had seized upon
and which had led him to the denial of all being.
Both men sought a way out of the contradictori-
ness and disparity of a double world order. The
leap into the indefinite, un-defineable, by which
Anaximander had once and for all escaped the
realm of come-to-be and its empirically given
qualities, did not come easy to minds as inde-

pendent as those of Heraclitus and Parmenides.
They sought to stay on their feet as long as
they could, preserving their leap for the spot
where the foot no longer finds support and one
must jump to keep from falling. Both of them
looked repeatedly at just that world which Anaximander had condemned with such melancholy
and had declared as the place of wickedness and
simultaneously of atonement for the unjustness
of all coming-to-be. Gazing at this world, Heraclitus, as we have seen, discovered what wonderful order, regularity and certainty manifested
themselves in all coming-to-be; from this he concluded that coming-to-be itself could not be anything evil or unjust. His look was oriented from
a point of view totally different from that of
Parmenides. The latter compared the qualities
and believed that he found them not equal, but
divided into two rubrics. Comparing, for example, light and dark, he found the latter obviously but the *negation* of the former. Thus he
differentiated between positive and negative qualities, seriously attempting to find and note this
basic contradictory principle throughout all nature. His method was as follows: he took several
contradictories, light and heavy for example, rare
and dense, active and passive, and held them
against his original model contradictories light
and dark. Whatever corresponded to light was
the positive quality, whatever corresponded to
dark, the negative. Taking heavy and light, for
example, light [in the sense of 'weightless'] was
apportioned to light, heavy to dark, and thus
heavy seemed to him but the negation of weight-

less, but weightlessness seemed a positive quality. The very method exhibits a defiant talent for abstract-logical procedure, closed against all influences of sensation. For heaviness surely seems to urge itself upon the senses as a positive quality; yet this did not prevent Parmenides from labelling it as a negation. Likewise he designated earth as against fire, cold as against warm, dense as against rare, feminine as against masculine, and passive as against active, to be negatives. Thus before his gaze our empirical world divided into two separate spheres, the one characterized by light, fieriness, warmth, weightlessness, rarification, activity and masculinity, and the other by the opposite, negative qualities. The latter really express only the lack, the absence of the former, positive ones. Thus he described the sphere which lacks the positive qualities as dark, earthy, cold, heavy, dense, and feminine-passive in general. Instead of the words "positive" and "negative" he used the absolute terms "existent" and "nonexistent." Now he had arrived at the principle—Anaximander notwithstanding—that this world of ours contains something which is existent, as well as something which is nonexistent. The existent should therefore not be sought outside the world and beyond our horizon. Right here before us, everywhere, in all coming-to-be, there is contained an active something which is existent.

But now he was left with the task of formulating a more exact answer to the question "What *is* coming-to-be?" And this was the moment when he had to leap to keep from falling, although

for natures such as Parmenides' perhaps all leap-
ing constitutes a kind of falling. Suffice it to say
that we shall enter the fog, the mysticism of
qualitates occultae and even, just a little, the
realm of mythology. Parmenides, like Heraclitus,
gazes at universal coming-to-be and at impermanence, and he can interpret passing-away only as
though it were a fault of nonexistence. For how
could the existent be guilty of passing away! But
coming-to-be, too, must be produced with the
help of the nonexistent, for the existent is always there. Of and by itself it could not come-
to-be nor could it explain coming-to-be. Hence
coming-to-be as well as passing-away would seem
to be produced by the negative qualities. But
since that which comes-to-be has a content which
is lost in the process of passing-away, it presupposes that the positive qualities (for they are
the essence of such content) likewise participate
in both processes of change. In brief, we now
have the dictum that "For coming-to-be, the
existent as well as the nonexistent are necessary;
whenever they interact, we have coming-to-be."
But how are the positive and the negative to
get together? Should they not forever flee each
other, as contradictories, and thus make all coming-to-be impossible? Here Parmenides appeals
to a *qualitas occulta*, to the mystic tendency of
opposites to attract and unite, and he symbolizes
the opposition in the name of Aphrodite and the
empirically well-known relationship between
masculinity and femininity. It is the power of
Aphrodite that weds the opposites, the existent
with the nonexistent. Desire unites the contradic-

tory and mutually repellent elements: the result
is coming-to-be. When desire is satiated, hatred
and inner opposition drives the existent and the
nonexistent apart once more—and man says,
"All things pass."

10

But no one lays hands with impunity on such
fearsome abstractions as "the existent" and "the
nonexistent." Slowly, upon touching them, the
blood congeals. There came the day when a
strange insight befell Parmenides, an insight
which seemed to withdraw the value from all his
old combinations so that he felt like throwing
them away like a bag of old worn-out coins. It
is usually assumed that an external influence, in
addition to the inwardly compelling consistency
of such terms as "existent" and "nonexistent"
shared in the invention of that fateful day. This
external event is supposed to be Parmenides' acquaintance with the theology of that ancient far-
travelled rhapsodist, singer of mystic nature dei-
fication, the Colophonian *Xenophanes*. Throughout an extraordinary lifetime, Xenophanes lived
as a travelling poet and through his travels became a widely informed and widely informa-
tive person who understood how to ask questions and tell stories. Heraclitus counted him

among the polyhistorians and among "historical" natures in general, in the sense already alluded to. Whence and when he picked up the mystical tendency toward the one, and the "one forever at rest," no one can now reconstruct. Perhaps it was the concept of an old man finally settled down, one before whose soul there appeared, after all the mobility of his wanderings and after all his restless learning and looking, the highest and greatest thing of all, a vision of divine rest, of the permanence of all things within a pantheistic archetypal peace. To me, by the way, it seems no more than accidental that in the same place, in Elea, two men should be living for a while who both carried in their minds a concept of unity. They did not form a school; they had nothing in common which one might have learned from the other and then passed along to others in turn. For the origin of their concepts of unity was a totally different one in each case, a downright opposite one in fact. If one of them did know the doctrine of the other, he would have had to translate it into a language of his own, even to understand it. But even in such translation the specific import of each would surely have been lost. Whereas Parmenides came to the unity of the existent purely by adherence to his supposed logic, spinning it out of the concepts of being and nonbeing, Xenophanes was a religious mystic who with his mystic unity belongs very typically to the sixth century. Even though he was not as cataclysmic a personality as Pythagoras, he shared his tendency and compulsion to improve human beings, to cleanse and to heal them, as he wandered from place to place. He is the teacher of ethics, though still on the rhapsodic level; in later times he would have been a Sophist. In his bold disapproval of the current mores and values he has not his equal in Greece. And to disapprove, he by no means withdraws into solitude, like Heraclitus and Plato, but stands up before the very public whose jubilant admiration of Homer, whose passionate yearning for the honors of the gymnastic festivals, whose worship of anthropomorphic stones he scourged wrathfully and scornfully, yet not in the quarrelsome fashion of a Thersites. The freedom of the individual finds its high point in Xenophanes, and it is in this almost boundless withdrawal from all conventionality that he is related more closely to Parmenides, not in that ultimate divine unity which he once saw in a vision befitting his century and which has hardly the expression or terminology in common with Parmenides' one being, not to mention origin.

It was rather an opposite frame of mind in which Parmenides found his doctrine of being. On a certain day and in a certain frame of mind he tested his two interactive contradictories, whose mutual desire and hatred constitute the world and all coming-to-be. He tested the existent and the nonexistent, the positive and the negative properties—and suddenly he found that he could not get past the concept of a negative quality, the concept of non-existence. Can something which is not be a quality? Or, more basically, can something which is not, be? For the only single form of knowledge which we trust immediately and absolutely and to deny which amounts to insanity is the tautology A = A. But just this tautological insight proclaims inexorably: What is not, is not. What is, is. And suddenly Parmenides felt a monstrous logical sin burdening his whole previous life. Had he not light-heartedly always assumed that there *are* such things as negative qualities, nonexistent entities, that, in other words, A is not A? But only total perversity of thinking could have done so. To be sure, he reflected, the great mass of people had always made the same perverse judgment; he had merely participated in a universal crime against logic. But the same moment that shows him his crime illuminates him with a glorious discovery. He has found a principle, the key to the cosmic secret, remote from all human illusion. Now, grasping the firm and awful hand of tautological truth about being, he can climb down, into the abyss of all things.

On his way down he meets Heraclitus—an unhappy encounter. Caring now for nothing except the strictest separation of being from nonbeing, he must hate in his deepest soul the antinomy-play of Heraclitus. Propositions such as "We are and at the same time are not," or "Being and nonbeing is at the same time the same and not the same," tangle and cloud everything which he had just illuminated and distinguished. They drove him to fury. "Away with those people," he screamed, "who seem to have two heads and yet know nothing. Everything is in flux with them, including their thinking. They stand in dull astonishment before things and yet must be deaf as well as blind to mix up the opposites the way they do!" The irrationality of the masses, glorified in playful antinomies and lauded as the culmination of all wisdom was now a painful and incomprehensible experience.

And then he really dipped into the cold bath of his awe-inspiring abstractions. That which truly is must be forever present; you cannot say of it "it was," "it will be." The existent cannot have come to be, for out of what could it have come? Out of the nonexistent? But the nonexistent is not, and cannot produce anything. Out of the existent? This would reproduce nothing but itself. It is the same with passing-away. Passing away is just as impossible as coming-to-be, as is all change, all decrease, all increase. In fact the only valid proposition that can be stated is "Everything of which you can say 'it has been' or 'it will be' is not; of the existent you can never say 'it is not.' " The existent is indivisible, for where is the second power that could divide it? It is immobile, for where could it move to? It can be neither infinitely large nor infinitely small, for it is perfect, and a perfectly given infinity is a contradiction. Thus it hovers: bounded, finished, immobile, everywhere in balance, equally perfect at each point, like a globe, though not in space, for this space would be a second existent. But there cannot be several existents. For in order to separate them, there would have to be something which is not existent, a supposition which cancels itself. Thus there is only eternal unity.

And now, whenever Parmenides glances backward at the world of come-to-be, the world whose existence he used to try to comprehend by means of ingenious conjectures, he becomes angry with his eyes for so much as seeing come-to-be, with his ears for hearing it. "Whatever you do, do not be guided by your dull eyes," is now his imperative, "nor by your resounding ears, nor by your tongue, but test all things with the power of your thinking alone." Thus he accomplished the immensely significant first critique of man's apparatus of knowledge, a critique as yet inadequate but doomed to bear dire consequences. By wrenching apart the senses and the capacity for abstraction, in other words by splitting up mind as though it were composed of two quite separate capacities, he demolished intellect itself, encouraging man to indulge in that wholly erroneous distinction between "spirit" and "body" which, especially since Plato, lies upon philosophy like a curse. All sense perceptions, says Parmenides, yield but illusions. And their main illusoriness lies in their pretense that the non-existent coexists with the existent, that Becoming, too, has Being. All the manifold colorful world known to experience, all the transformations of its qualities, all the orderliness of its ups and downs, are cast aside mercilessly as mere semblance and illusion. Nothing may be learned from them. All effort spent upon this false deceitful world which is futile and negligible, faked into a lying existence by the senses is therefore wasted. When one makes as total a judgment as does Parmenides about the whole of the world, one

ceases to be a scientist, an investigator into any of
the world's parts. One's sympathy toward phenomena atrophies; one even develops a hatred
for phenomena including oneself, a hatred for
being unable to get rid of the everlasting deceit-
fulness of sensation. Henceforward truth shall
live only in the palest, most abstracted generali-
ties, in the empty husks of the most indefinite
terms, as though in a house of cobwebs. And beside such truth now sits our philosopher, likewise as bloodless as his abstractions, in the spun
out fabric of his formulas. A spider at least wants
blood from its victims. The Parmenidean philosopher hates most of all the blood of his victims, the blood of the empirical reality which
was sacrificed and shed by him.

11

And this was a Greek who flourished approxi-
mately during the outbreak of the Ionian Revolt.
In those days it was possible for a Greek to flee
from an over-abundant reality as though it were
but the tricky scheming of the imagination—and
to flee, not like Plato into the land of eternal
ideas, into the workshop of the world-creator,
feasting one's eyes on the unblemished unbreak-
able archetypes, but into the rigor mortis of the
coldest emptiest concept of all, the concept of

being. Let us be exceedingly careful not to interpret such a remarkable event according to
false analogies. The Parmenidean escape was not
the flight from the world taken by the Hindu
philosophers; it was not evoked by a profound
religious conviction as to the depravity, ephemerality and accursedness of human existence. Its
ultimate goal, peace in being, was not striven
after as though it were the mystic absorption into
one all-sufficing ecstatic state of mind which is
the enigma and vexation of ordinary minds.
Parmenides' thinking conveys nothing whatever
of the dark intoxicating fragrance of Hindu wisdom which is not entirely absent from Pythagoras and Empedocles. No, the strange thing
about his philosophic feat at this period is just
its lack of fragrance, of color, soul, and form, its
total lack of blood, religiosity and ethical
warmth. What astonishes us is the degree of
schematism and abstraction (in a Greek!), above
all, the terrible energetic striving for *certainty*
in an epoch which otherwise thought mythically
and whose imagination was highly mobile and
fluid. "Grant me, ye gods, but one certainty,"
runs Parmenides' prayer, "and if it be but a
log's breadth on which to lie, on which to ride
upon the sea of uncertainty. Take away everything that comes-to-be, everything lush, colorful,
blossoming, illusory, everything that charms and
is alive. Take all these for yourselves and grant
me but the one and only, poor empty certainty."

The prelude in Parmenides' philosophy is
played with ontology as its theme. Experience
nowhere offered him being as he imagined it, but

he concluded its existence from the fact that he
was able to think it. This is a conclusion which
rests on the assumption that we have an organ of
knowledge which reaches into the essence of
things and is independent of experience. The
content of our thinking, according to Parmenides, is not present in sense perception but
is an additive from somewhere else, from an
extra-sensory world to which we have direct ac-
cess by means of our thinking. Now Aristotle
asserted against all similar reasoning that existence is never an intrinsic part of essence. One
may never infer the *existentia* of being from the
concept being—whose *essentia* is nothing more
than being itself. The logical truth of the pair of
opposites being and nonbeing is completely empty, if the object of which it is a reflection cannot be given, i.e., the sense perception from
which this antithesis was abstracted. Without
such derivation from a perception, it is no more
than a playing with ideas, which in fact yields no
knowledge. For the mere logical criterion of
truth, as Kant teaches it, the correspondence of
knowledge with the universal and formal laws
of understanding and reason, is, to be sure, the
conditio sine qua non, the negative condition of
all truth. But further than this, logic cannot go,
and the error as to content rather than form
cannot be detected by using any logical touchstone whatever. As soon as we seek the content
of the logical truth of the paired propositions
"What is, is; what is not, is not," we cannot indeed find any reality whatever which is con-
str ted strictly in accordance with those proposi-

tions. I may say of a tree that "it is" in distinction to things which are not trees; I may say "it is coming to be" in distinction to itself seen at a different time; I may even say "it is not," as for example in "it is not yet a tree" when I am looking at a shrub. Words are but symbols for the relations of things to one another and to us; nowhere do they touch upon absolute truth. Above all, the word "being" designates only the most general relationship which connects all things, as does the word "nonbeing." But if the existence of things themselves cannot be proved, surely the inter-relationship of things, their so-called being or nonbeing, will advance us not a step toward the land of truth. Through words and concepts we shall never reach beyond the wall of relations, to some sort of fabulous primal ground of things. Even in the pure forms of sense and understanding, in space, time and causality, we gain nothing that resembles an eternal verity. It is absolutely impossible for a subject to see or have insight into something while leaving itself out of the picture, so impossible that knowing and being are the most opposite of all spheres. And if Parmenides could permit himself, in the uninformed naiveté of his time, so far as critique of the intellect is concerned, to derive absolute being from a forever subjective concept, today, after Kant, it is certainly reckless ignorance to attempt it. Now and again, particularly among badly taught theologians who would like to play philosopher, the task of philosophy is designated as "comprehending the absolute by means of consciousness," even in the form of "The absolute is already present, how could it otherwise be sought?" (Hegel) or "Being must be given to us somehow, must be somehow attainable; if it were not we could not have the concept." (Beneke) The concept of being! As though it did not show its low empirical origin in its very etymology! For *esse* basically means "to breathe." And if man uses it of all things other than himself as well, he projects his conviction that he himself breathes and lives by means of a metaphor, i.e., a non-logical process, upon all other things. He comprehends their existence as a "breathing" by analogy with his own. The original meaning of the word was soon blurred, but enough remains to make it obvious that man imagines the existence of other things by analogy with his own existence, in other words anthropomorphically and in any event, with non-logical projection. But even for man—quite aside from his projection—the proposition "I breathe, therefore being exists" is wholly insufficient. The same objection must be made against it as must be made against *ambulo, ergo sum* or *ergo est.*

12

The second concept, of more content than being, likewise invented by Parmenides though not used by him as skillfully as by his disciple

Zeno, is that of the infinite. Nothing infinite can exist, for to assume it would yield the contradictory concept of a perfect infinity. Now since our reality, our given world, everywhere bears the stamp of just such perfect infinity, the word signifies in its very nature a contradiction to logic and hence to the real, and is therefore an illusion, a lie, a phantasm. Zeno especially makes use of indirect proof. He says, for example, "There can be no movement from one place to another, for if there were such movement, we would have a perfect infinity, but this is an impossibility. Achilles cannot catch up with the tortoise which has a small start over him, for in order to reach even the starting point of the tortoise, Achilles must have traversed innumerable, infinitely many spaces: first half of the interval, then a fourth of it, an eighth, a sixteenth, and so on *ad infinitum*. If he in reality does catch up with the tortoise, this is an un-logical phenomenon, not a real one. It is not true Being; it is merely an illusion. For it is never possible to finish the infinite." Another popular device of this doctrine is the example of the flying and yet resting arrow. At each moment of its flight it occupies a position. In this position it is at rest. But can we say that the sum of infinitely many positions of rest is identical with motion? Can we say that resting, infinitely repeated, equals motion, which is its contrary? The infinite is here utilized as the catalyst of reality; in its presence reality dissolves. If the concepts are firm, eternal and existent (remembering that being and thinking coincide for Parmenides), if in other words the infinite can never be complete, if rest can never become motion, then the arrow has really never flown at all. It never left its initial position of rest; no moment of time has passed. Or, to express it differently: in this so-called, but merely alleged reality, there is really neither time nor space nor motion. Finally, even the arrow itself is an illusion, for it has its origin in the many, in the sense-produced phantasmagoria of the non-one. Let us assume that the arrow has true being. Then it would be immobile, timeless, uncreated, rigid and eternal—which is impossible to conceive. Let us assume that motion is truly real. Then there would be no rest, hence no position for the arrow, hence no space—which is impossible to conceive. Let us assume that time is real. Then it could not be infinitely divisible. The time that the arrow needs would have to consist of a limited number of moments; each of these moments would have to be an *atomon*—which is impossible to conceive. All our conceptions lead to contradictions as soon as their empirically given content, drawn from our perceivable world, is taken as an eternal verity. If absolute motion exists, then space does not; if absolute space exists, then motion does not; if absolute being exists, then the many does not. Wouldn't one think that confronted with such logic a man would attain the insight that such concepts do not touch the heart of things, do not undo the tangle of reality? Parmenides and Zeno, on the contrary, hold fast to the truth and universal validity of the concepts and discard the perceiva-

ble world as the antithesis to all true and univer-
sally valid concepts, as the objectification of
illogic and contradiction. The starting point of
all their proof is the wholly unprovable, im-
probable assumption that with our capacity to
form concepts we possess the decisive and highest
criterion as to being and nonbeing, i.e., as to objective reality and its antithesis. Instead of being
corrected and tested against reality (considering
that they are in fact derived from it) the concepts, on the contrary, are supposed to measure
and direct reality and, in case reality contradicts
logic, to condemn the former. In order to impose
upon the concepts this capacity for judging
reality, Parmenides had to ascribe to them the
being which was for him the only true being.
Thinking and that single uncreated perfect
globe of existentiality were not to be compre-
hended as two different types of being, since of
course there could be no dichotomy in being.
Thus an incredibly bold notion became necessary, the notion of the identity of thinking and
being. No form of perception, no symbol, no
allegory could help here; the notion was utterly
beyond conceiving, but—it was necessary. In its
very lack of any and all possibility for being
translated into sensation, it celebrated the highest triumph over the world and the claims of the
senses. Thinking and that bulbous-spherical being, wholly dead-inert and rigid-immobile must,
according to Parmenides' imperative, coincide
and be utterly the same thing. What a shock to
human imagination! But let their identity con-

tradict sensation! Just that fact guarantees better
than anything else that this was a conception
not derived from the senses.

13

One might advance against Parmenides a
sturdy pair of *argumenta ad hominem* or *ex con-
cessis*. They would not bring the truth to light,
to be sure, though they do expose the falsehood
inherent in the absolute separation of senses and
concepts, and in the identity of being and thinking. In the first place: if thinking in concepts, on
the part of reason, is real, then the many and
motion must partake of reality also, for reasoned
thinking is mobile. It moves from concept to concept. It is mobile, in other words, within a plurality of realities. Against this, no objection can be
made; it is quite impossible to designate thinking as a rigid persistence, as an eternally unmoved thinking-in-and-on-itself on the part of a
unity. In the second place: if only fraud and
semblance emanate from the senses, and if in
truth there is only the real identity of being and
thinking, what then are the senses themselves?
Evidently a part of semblance, since they do not
coincide with thinking, and since their product,
the sensuous world, does not coincide with semblance. But if the senses are semblance, to whom

do they dissemble? How, being unreal, can they deceive? Nonbeing cannot even practice deceit. Therefore the whence of illusion and semblance remains an enigma, in fact a contradiction. We shall call these two *argumenta ad hominem* one, the argument based on the mobility of reason; two, the argument based on the origin of semblance. From the first follows the reality of motion and of the many, from the second the impossibility of Parmenidean semblance. In both cases, we are still accepting Parmenides' main doctrine concerning being as well-founded. But this doctrine merely states, "The existent alone has being; the nonexistent does not." Now if motion has being, then what is true of being in general and in all cases is true of motion: it is uncreated, eternal, indestructible, without increase or decrease. But if semblance is denied of this world (by means of the question as to its origin), if the stage of so-called coming-to-be, of change —in other words our whole multi-formed restless colorful and rich existence—is protected against Parmenidean discard, then it is necessary to characterize this world of interaction and transformation as a *sum* of such truly existent essences, existing simultaneously in all eternity. In this supposition too there is no room for transformation in a narrow sense, i.e., for coming-to-be. But what we have now is a multiplicity which has true being; all the properties have true being, as has motion. About each and every moment of this world, even if we choose moments that lie a millenium apart, one would have to be able to say: all true essences contained in the world are exist-

ent simultaneously, unchanged, undiminished,
without increase, without decrease. A millenium
later exactly the same holds true; nothing has
meanwhile changed. If, in spite of this, the world
looks totally different from time to time, this is
not an illusion, not mere semblance, but rather
the consequence of everlasting motion. True
being is moved sometimes this way, sometimes
that way, together asunder, upwardly downward,
withinly in all directions.

14

With such a conception we have already taken
a step into the field of *Anaxagoras'* teaching. He
raises both objections in all their full force
against Parmenides, that of the mobility of
thought as well as that of the origin of semblance.
But so far as Parmenides' main doctrine goes, he
kept Anaxagoras in submission to it, as he did all
subsequent philosophers and nature investigators. They all deny the possibility of coming-
to-be and passing-away, as ordinary people imagine it and as Anaximander and Heraclitus had
assumed it with more profound reflectivity, yet
still unreflectively. Such mythological origin in
nothingness, disappearance into nothingness,
such arbitrary transformation of nothing into
something, such random exchange, doffing and

donning of qualities was from now on taken to be nonsensical, but so was, and for the same reasons, the origin of the many in the one, of manifold qualities in the one primal quality, in short the whole derivation of the world from a single primal substance as Thales and Heraclitus had taught it. Now a particular problem had been set up, the problem of transferring the doctrine of the uncreated and imperishable being to the world as it is here and now, without having recourse to the theory of semblance with its deceit practiced upon us by the senses. But if the empirical world is not to be semblance, if matter is not to be derived from either nothing or from some single something, then matter itself must contain true being. Its substance and content must be unconditionally real, and all its changes can refer only to form, i.e., to position, order, grouping, mixing or separation of these forever simultaneously existing essences. We have then the same situation as in a game of dice. The dice are always the same, but falling now this way, now that, they signify different things for us. All the older theories had gone back to a primal element as the womb and cause of coming-to-be, to water, air, fire, or Anaximander's indefinite. Against this Anaxagoras now asserts that the like can never produce the unlike and that change can never be explained out of a single existent. Whether one imagines the one assumed substance to be rarified or densified does not matter. One can never reach by means of rarification or densification what one desires to explain, namely the plurality of qualities. But if

the world is in fact full of many different qualities, then, if they are not semblance, they must
have being which means they must be forever
uncreated, imperishable and always simultaneously existent. Semblance they cannot be, since
the question as to the origin of semblance remains unanswered, in fact answers itself in the
negative. The older investigators had wanted to
simplify the problem of coming-to-be by positing
a single substance which would carry the possibility of all coming-to-be in its womb. Now, on
the contrary, it is said that there are countless
substances, but never more, never fewer, never
new ones. Only motion tumbles them about into
new patterns. And motion is truth and not semblance, as Anaxagoras proves in spite of Parmenides by the indubitable succession of ideas in
our thinking. In any event, the inert stable dead
being of Parmenides has been disposed of. Now
there are many existents, just as surely as all
these many existents (existences, substances) are
in motion. Change is motion—but where does
motion come from? Does motion perhaps leave
the true essence of those many independent isolated substances wholly untouched, and *must* it
therefore be alien to them, according to the strict
concept of that which is existent? Or does motion
nonetheless adhere to things themselves? We
stand before an important decision: according to
how we turn at this point, we shall enter upon
the field of Anaxagoras or Empedocles or Democritus. The critical question must be asked: if there
are many substances, and these many move, what
is it that moves them? Do they move each other?

Does gravity alone move them? Or are there magical forces of attraction or repulsion inherent in things themselves? Or does the impetus for motion lie outside of the many real substances? Or, to put the question more specifically: When two things show succession, a change of position relative to each other, does this change originate in them? And is this to be explained mechanically or magically? Or, if such is not the case, is there a third thing that moves them? It is a wicked problem. Parmenides, even if he were to admit a plurality of substances, would still be able to prove the impossibility of motion against Anaxagoras. He could say: Take two essences, each existent in itself with a totally different independently absolute being—and such are the Anaxagorian substances. With their nature as described, they can never collide, never move each other, never attract each other. There is no causality between them, no bridge; they do not touch one another, disturb one another, concern one another. Repulsion is then exactly as inexplicable as magical attraction between them. Whatever is totally absolutely alien to one another can in no wise exert influence upon one another, hence neither move nor be moved. Parmenides would even have added: The only recourse left to you is to ascribe motion to things themselves, but in that case everything that you know and see as motion is only an illusion and not true motion at all, for the only kind of motion proper to your unconditionally unique substances would be autonomous motion, devoid of all effect. But the very reason you are positing

motion to begin with is so that you can explain
the effects of interaction, of displacement in
space, of change—in brief, the causalities and
relations among things. But just these effects
would not be explained; they would remain just
as problematic as before, wherefore it is impossible to imagine why you find it necessary to
posit motion, since it does not do what you want
it to. Motion just does not accord with the essence of things. It remains forever alien to them.

To get past such argumentation, the opponents of the Eleatic unmoved unity were led
astray by a prejudice originating in sensation. It
seems so unarguable that every true existent is a
space-occuping body, a clump of material, large
or small, but in any case extended in space, so
that two or more such clumps cannot occupy
the same space. With such presupposition Anaxagoras, and later Democritus, assumed that the
clumps would have to collide if they should hit
one another as they moved around, that they
would contest for the same space, and that hence
it is this strife between the clumps which causes
all change. In other words those wholly isolated,
totally different, and forever unchanging substances were, after all, not thought of as absolutely different, but rather they were felt to have
a completely like substratum, a fragment of
space-filling matter, in addition to their specific,
wholly unique property. In their participation
in matter they were all equal and alike and
could therefore have an effect upon each other,
i.e., collide. All change, in fact, depended not at
all on the differences between substances but on

their similarity in so far as they all partake of matter. There is a logical error here inherent in Anaxagoras' presuppositions. For that which is truly existent in itself would have to be a wholly absolute unit, allowing no further assumptions as to its cause. But all the Anaxagorian substances have after all something which conditions them, namely a material substratum whose existence they posit. The substance "red" for example was for Anaxagoras not only red in itself but tacitly a fragment of property-less matter. Only with this latter part of it does "red as such" react upon other substances. Not with its aspect of redness but with that which is not red, not colored, in fact not qualitatively determined at all. If red were taken strictly as red, as the substance proper without a substratum, then Anaxagoras would surely not have dared to speak of an effect of red upon other substances, such as that "the red as such" transmits by impulse the motion received by "the flesh as such." It would then be clear that a true existent could never be moved.

15

One must look at the opponents of the Eleatics to appreciate the extraordinary advantages inherent in Parmenides' hypothesis. What embarrassments—which Parmenides escaped—awaited

Anaxagoras and all the others who believed in
a plurality of substances as soon as the question
of how many substances arises! Anaxagoras took
the leap, shut his eyes, and said "infinitely
many." This flight at any rate took him past the
unbelievably troublesome proof of a certain definite number of elemental substances. Since the
infinitely many would have to exist without increase, unchanged, in all eternity, the contradiction inherent in imagining a closed off and perfect infinity was already given in the hypothesis.
In brief, plurality, motion, infinity—all of them
chased off by Parmenides with his astonishing
proposition about being—now returned from
their exile, sniping at Parmenides' opponents
enough to cause those wounds which never heal.
Obviously the opponents have no sure awareness
of the frightful force of the Eleatic thoughts, e.g.,
"There can be no time, no motion, no space, for
we can only imagine all these to be infinite.
Whether infinitely large or infinitely divisible,
everything infinite has no being. It does not
exist." But no one who interprets the meaning
of the word "being" strictly, who takes the existence of a contradiction such as a finished infinity seriously as an impossibility, can doubt
this. But if actuality shows us everything solely
in the form of perfect infinity, then it is self-
evident that actuality contradicts itself, hence
has no true reality. And if the opponents wish
to interpose with something like "Your thinking
itself shows succession, hence your thinking cannot be real either and therefore cannot be used
for proving your point," then Parmenides might

have answered as Kant did in a similar case, to a similar objection. "I can say, to be sure, that my ideas follow one upon the other, but all that means is that I am conscious of them in terms of succession in time, i.e., according to the form of the inward sense. But this does not make time a thing which exists in itself, nor a condition objectively adhering to things." In other words what has to be distinguished here is pure think- ing, which is timeless like the one being of Par- menides, and our consciousness of this thinking. The latter comes already translated by thinking into the forms of semblance, i.e., into succession, multiplicity and motion. It is probable that this would have been Parmenides' way out, although the counter-argument would then be the same as A. Spir's argument against Kant (in *Denken und Wirklichkeit*. 2nd ed. Vol. I, pp. 209f):

> Now in the first place it is clear that I can know nothing of succession as such if I do not hold its successive stages simultaneously in my consciousness. The idea of succession, in other words, is not in itself successive; consequently it is completely different from the succession of ideas. In the second place, Kant's hypothesis implies such self-evident absurdities that one can only wonder how he could have left them out of account. Caesar and Socrates, according to his hypothesis, are not really dead. They are just as alive as they were two thousand years ago and only appear to be dead to an arrange- ment of my 'inward sense.' Men as yet unborn are already alive, and if they have not yet ap- peared on the scene this too is the fault of the arrangement of this inward sense. The main

question is this: how can the beginning and
the end of conscious life itself, together with
all its inward and outward senses, exist only
in the interpretation of the inward sense? The
actual fact is that one absolutely cannot deny
the reality of change. If you throw it out the
window it will slip back in through the key-
hole. One can say 'it merely seems to me that
conditions and ideas change,' but this semblance itself is something objectively given.
Within it, succession indubitably has objective
reality; within it something actually follows
upon something else.—Besides, it is necessary
to note that the entire critique of reason can
have its foundation and justification only in
the presupposition that our *ideas* appear to us
as they are. For even if they appeared to us as
other than they really are, one could not make
any valid assertions about them, hence produce
no epistemology and no 'transcendental' exami-
nation of objective validity. And it is beyond
all doubt that our ideas appear to us as suc-
cessive.

Contemplation of this doubtlessly certain succession and mobility now pushes Anaxagoras to
assume a remarkable hypothesis. Evidently the
ideas moved of themselves; they were not pushed
nor did they have any moving cause outside
them. Hence there is something, he says to himself, that carries in itself the origin and the beginning of motion. But then he notes, in the second place, that this idea moves not only itself
but that it moves something quite different from
itself. It moves the body. Thus he discovers,
through the most immediate experience, an ef-

fect on the part of ideas upon matter extended
in space, which may be recognized by the motion
of the latter. This seems to him to be a fact.
Only secondarily does he feel challenged to explain the fact. Enough, he now has a regulative
scheme for motion in the world which he now
thinks of as either a movement of the true isolated essences by means of the faculty of ideas,
the *nous*, or else as motion by means of something already moved. That the latter view, the
mechanical transmission of movements and impulses, likewise contains a problem, assuming his
basic presupposition, probably escaped him. The
common-place every-day nature of effectuation
by means of impulse probably dulled his eye for
the enigma which it presents. He did, on the
other hand, sense quite well the problematic not
to say contradictory nature of the effect of ideas
upon substances existent in themselves. This is
why he sought to derive such effect from a
mechanical shoving and pushing phenomenon
which seemed explicable and factual to him. The
nous, in any event, was also such a substance existent in itself, and was characterized by him as
an extremely delicate sensitive material with the
specific property of "thinking." With such an
assumed character then, the effect of such matter
upon other matter had to be of exactly the same
sort as the effect exerted by another substance
upon a third, i.e., a mechanical one, moving by
means of pressures and impulses. In any case, he
now had a substance which moves itself and
other things as well, whose motion does not come
from outside and does not depend on anything

else. It then seemed almost a matter of indif-
ference how this self-caused motion was to be
imagined. Perhaps something like the back and
forth movement of very tiny delicate round drop-
lets of mercury. Among all the questions dealing
with motion, none is more annoying than the
one which asks for its starting point. For though
one may imagine all the other movements as
causes and effects, the one original primal motion has still to be explained. For mechanical
movements, in any event, the first link of the
chain cannot be sought in a mechanical movement since this would mean falling back on the
contradictory concept of a *causa sui*. But to in-
vest eternally absolute things with a motion of
their own, as a sort of aboriginal endowment,
does not work either. For motion is not to be
imagined as devoid of some direction whence
and whereupon; it must be imagined as a rela-
tion or condition, in other words. But a thing is
no longer existent in itself and absolute if in its
very nature it necessarily refers to something
existent outside itself. Faced with this embar-
rassment, Anaxagoras thought he had found an
extraordinary aid and salvation in that *nous,*
self-moving and otherwise independent. Its nature seems just obscure and veiled enough to
deceive one as to the fact that to assume it, too,
involves at bottom that forbidden *causa sui*. So
far as empirical observation is concerned, it is
quite settled that ideas are not *causa sui* but ef-
fected by the physical brain. Empirically speaking, it seems curiously eccentric, in fact, to separate the "spirit," the brain-product, from its

causa and to imagine its continued existence after such separation. But that is what Anaxagoras did; he forgot the brain, its astonishingly elaborate refinement, the delicacy and convolutedness of its labyrinths, and instead decreed the "spirit as such." This "spirit as such" had choice—a magnificent discovery! At some unspecified time it had the capacity of beginning, of moving things that lay outside itself; on the other hand it was capable of concerning itself with itself alone for enormously long stretches of time. In short, Anaxagoras could now assume a *first* moment of motion in primeval time, as the germination point of all so-called "becoming," i.e., of all change, i.e., of all displacement and shifting of the eternal substances and their particles. Even though spirit itself is eternal, it is nonetheless not compelled to torture itself for aeons with the pushing and manipulating of little kernels of matter. In any case there was a time and a condition of matter—regardless whether of long or short duration—when *nous* had not yet influenced it, when matter was still inert. This is the period of Anaxagorian chaos.

16

The Anaxagorian chaos is not a conception whose advantages are instantly seen. To compre-

hend it, one must have understood the idea
which our philosopher had formed about so-called
coming-to-be. For taken in itself, the condition of
all the various elemental existences before motion would not necessarily produce an absolute
mixture of all the seeds of things, as Anaxagoras
expressed himself, a mixture which he imagined
as a total pell-mell of even the tiniest particles,
the result of mixing, as though with mortar and
pestle, all the elemental substances until they
were like dust motes and could be stirred about
in the chaos as though in a mixing-cup. One
might say that this is not a necessary conception
of chaos, that one might just as well assume a
random position of all the existent substances
instead of an infinite separation of all their parts.
Irregular juxtaposition, one can argue, would
suffice; there is no need for a pell-mell mixture,
much less one which is imagined to be so utterly
total. How then did Anaxagoras arrive at such
a difficult and complicated idea? Through his
particular understanding, as we have said, of "becoming" as it is given in empirical experience.
He drew from experience first a highly unusual
proposition as to becoming, and in its wake his
doctrine of chaos was forced to appear on the
scene.

Observation of the productive processes of nature, rather than consideration of any former
philosophical system, gave Anaxagoras the doctrine that *everything originates from everything.*
This was his scientific conviction, based on a
manifold induction which was, at bottom, necessarily boundlessly meagre. His proof ran as fol-

lows: if opposite could be shown to arise from opposite, black for example from white, then everything is possible. And this actually happens when white snow dissolves into black water. He explained nutrition to himself by assuming invisibly small component portions of flesh or blood or bone which separate out in the process of nutrition and combine with their likes in the body. But if everything can come-to-be from everything, solid from liquid, hard from soft, black from white, flesh from bread, then everything must be contained in everything as well. In such a case the names of things express only a preponderance of one substance over the others which are also present, only in smaller, often not even perceptible amounts. Contained in gold, i.e., in that which *a potiore* we designate by the name "gold," there must be also silver, snow, bread and flesh, but only in very small shares; the whole is named for its preponderance of gold-substance.

Now how is it possible that one substance preponderates and fills a thing with more of its mass than do other substances? Experience shows that such preponderance is produced gradually by motion that it is the result of a process commonly called coming-to-be. The fact, on the other hand, that everything is contained in everything, is not the result of such a process but on the contrary is the presupposition of all coming-to-be and all being-moved. Hence it precedes all coming-to-be. In other words, empiricism teaches that like is constantly added to like—as in nutrition for example. Hence it was originally not contained in the same thing, not clumped together but separated. In the empirical processes that are before our very eyes, like is constantly drawn out of unlike and moved elsewhere (e.g., the flesh particles in nutrition are drawn out of bread and added onto flesh). Hence the pell-mell of the various substances is the older form of the constitution of things, taking place in time before all "becoming" and moving. If thus all so-called becoming is an elimination and presupposes a mixture, the question is what degree of mixed-ness the original pell-mell mixture must have had. Although the process is a movement of like toward like and as a process has already lasted an enormously long time, one nonetheless can recognize even now that remainders and seeds of all things are contained in all things, and that they are waiting there to be eliminated, to be separated out. Only here and there a preponderance has been achieved. Hence the primal mixture must have been total and complete, i.e., applicable to the infinitely small, since the demixing is taking infinite time. In all this, Anaxagoras adheres strictly to the thought that everything that possesses essential being is divisible infinitely without losing its property as a specific.

After such presuppositions, Anaxagoras imagines the primal existence of the world to be something like a dust-like mass of infinitely small filled points, each of which is a single specific, possessing but one property, yet in such fashion that each specific property is represented in infinitely many single points. Aristotle called these points *"homoeomeries"* in consideration of the fact that they are the like parts of a whole which is like its parts. But it would be a great error to equate the primal pell-mell of all such points (such "seeds of things") with the single primal substance of Anaximander. For the latter, called the "indefinite," is an absolutely single and unique mass, the former an aggregate of substances. One may, to be sure, say the same things of the aggregate that one can say of Anaximander's indefinite. Aristotle does so; he says it can neither be white nor grey nor black nor any color whatever; it is tasteless, odorless and, generally and as a whole, neither quantitatively nor qualitatively determined. Thus far one can equate the Anaximandrian indefinite with the Anaxagorian primal mixture. But aside from these similarities, which are negative, they can be distinguished on the positive side in that the primal mixture is a composite, the indefinite a unity. Anaxagoras, with the assumption of his chaos, had at least this advantage over Anaximander, that he did not have to derive the many from the one or coming-to-be from being.

He did, to be sure, have to admit to one exception in his total mixture of seeds; *nous* was not in primeval times nor is it now admixed to any thing. For if it were mixed into so much as a single existent, it would have to dwell in all things, in infinitely divided portions. This exception is logically highly suspect, especially considering the material nature of *nous* as described earlier. There is something mythological about it, and it looks arbitrary; yet according to the Anaxagorian premises, it is a strict necessity.

Spirit is infinitely divisible, by the way, like any other substance. But it is not divisible by other substances, only by itself. When it divides and, dividing, clumps now into large fragments, now into smaller ones, it retains its original mass and quality and has done so in all eternity. That which at the present moment is spirit in the whole world, in animals, plants and men, is the same thing that it was a thousand years ago, although distributed differently. But wherever spirit is related to another substance, it is never admixed, but instead seizes the alien substance voluntarily. It moves and displaces it by free choice; in other words, spirit controls it. Spirit, which alone has motion in itself, is the sole possessor of autonomy in the world. It demonstrates this by moving the substance-kernels about. But where does it move them? Or is motion without direction, without ascertainable course thinkable? Does spirit act as randomly in its impulses as its timing is random? In other words, does accident, which is to say the blindest caprice, rule within motion? It is at this borderline that we step into the holy of holies of Anaxagoras' field of ideas.

17

What had to be accomplished in that chaotic pell-mell of primeval conditions, before all motion, so that the world as it now is might come-to-be, with its times of day and times of year, all conforming to law, with its manifold beauty and order, all without the addition of any new substances or force? How in other words could a chaos become a cosmos? This can only be the consequence of motion but it must be a definite and a wisely instituted motion. Such a motion is the means employed by the *nous;* its end would be the complete separating out of the likes, an end which is still unattained, since the disorder and state of mixture at the beginning was of infinite magnitude. The end can only be striven toward in an enormously long process; it cannot be created all at once by a mythological magic wand. When someday, at an infinitely remote time, it is accomplished, when all the likes are gathered together and the primal essences lie side by side, undivided and in beautiful order, when each tiny particle has found its companions and its home, when the great peace enters the world after the great divisions and splits of the substances and no more split or divided material is left—then *nous* shall return to its self-movement, no longer roaming the world, itself divided, at times into greater, at times into smaller masses, as vegetative or animal spirit, indwelling in alien materials. Meanwhile the task is not yet at an end, but the kind of motion that the *nous* has figured out, in order to accomplish its end, demonstrates marvellous efficiency, for by it the task is nearer completion with each passing moment. For it is characterized by a spiralling movement. It began at some random point of the chaotic mixture, in the form of a small turn, and in ever greater orbits this circular movement spans all available being, by its centrifugal force pulling out all likes to join their likes. First, the rolling gyrations join the dense to the dense, the rare to the rare, and likewise the dark, the light, the moist, the dry to join their likes; beyond these general rubrics there are two more comprehensive classifications: aether, i.e., everything that is warm, light and rare, and air, designating everything dark, cold, heavy and solid. In the separation of the aethereal masses from the aerial ones, the next effect of the wheel that is rolling in ever larger circles is something like the eddy created by someone standing in a non-moving body of water. The heavy components are forced into the center and are compressed. In the same way, the travelling water-spout in chaos forms along its outside a concentration of its ethereal, thin light components, along its inside the cloudy, heavy, moist ones. Then, continuing the process, the aerial mass within separates out first its water, then the earthy component out of the water, then, out of the earthy, with the help of the terrible cold pervading it, the minerals. But now and again some of the mineral masses are wrenched sidewise off the earth by the momentum of the revolutions and cast into the realm of hot bright aether. There the fiery element brings them to a red-hot glow and swings them along with its own circular movement, thus causing them to radiate light. As the sun and the stars, they now illuminate and warm the dark and cold earth.

The entire conception has a marvellous boldness and simplicity and nothing at all of that clumsy and anthropomorphic teleology that Anaxagoras is frequently accused of. His conception has its grandeur and its proud accomplishment in the fact that he derives the entire cosmos of "becoming" from the moving circle, whereas Parmenides had looked upon true existence as though it were a motionless dead globe. Once Anaxagoras' circle is moved, once *nous* has started it on its revolutions, all order, all conformity to law and all beauty of the world are but the natural consequences of that first impulse to move. What an injustice we do Anaxagoras when we complain of his wisely reserved use of teleology in his cosmic conception and scornfully talk about his *nous* as though it were a *deus ex machina*. Quite on the contrary, Anaxagoras could have used words as proud as Kant's (in his General Natural History and Theory of the Heavens) to take credit for the disposal of mythological and theistic miraculous interventions and anthropomorphic purposes and utilities. Is it not a sublime thought, to derive the magnificence of the cosmos and the marvellous arrangements of the stellar orbits wholly from a single, simple, purely mechanical movement, from a mathematical figure in motion, as it were! Instead of seeing in it the intentions and the intervening hands of a machine-god, he derived it from a type of oscillation which, once having begun, is necessary and predictable in its course and attains effects which are the equal of the wisest calculations of ratiocination, and of the utmost planning of purposiveness—but without being them. "I am enjoying the pleasure," said Kant, "of seeing a well-ordered totality creating itself, without the aid of arbitrary fictions, only by the impulse of ordered laws of motion, which is so similar to that world system which is our own, that I cannot keep from taking it to be the same. It seems to me that one might say at this point, without presumption, 'Give me materiality and I shall build a world from it!' "

18

Now, however, even assuming that the primal mixture has been properly understood, there seem to be some doubts about the grand scheme of universe-creation which arises from its mechanics. Even if spirit causes the start of circular movement at some spot or other, nonetheless its continuation is still hard to imagine, especially since it is supposed to be infinite and eventually to whirl around every one of the available masses. One might guess, at the very outset, that the pressure of all the as yet disordered materials would choke the hardly begun tiny revolution. Since this does not happen, however, we must presuppose that the impelling *nous* starts suddenly, with frightful force—so fast, in any event, that we must call its motion a "whirl." This is how Democritus, too, described it. Since such a whirl must be infinitely strong in order not to be stopped by the load of the entire infinite world that is resting on it, it must be infinitely rapid, for strength can originally demonstrate itself only in the form of speed. The wider the concentric rings grow, the slower the movement may become. When motion shall have reached the end of, the infinite world, at long last, it must needs have attained an infinitely low speed of revolution. Conversely, if we imagine the motion infinitely large, i.e., infinitely fast—as we have to, at the very first inception of movement—then the starting circle must have been infinitely small. Hence we get, for the beginning, a point rotating about itself with an infinitely small material content. But such a point could not explain any further movement; one could easily imagine each and every point of the primal mass whirling around itself, yet leaving the mass as a whole unmoved and unseparated. But if the material point of infinite smallness that is originally seized and whirled by the *nous* was not, as a matter of fact, rotated around itself, but instead described a periphery which was randomly chosen as larger than itself, then this alone would suffice to impel other material points, to move them onward, to centrifuge them, rebound them, and thus spread a tumult which would create as its first product the separation of the aerial from the aethereal masses. Just as the inception of movement, then, is a voluntary act of *nous,* so is the quality of its inception, insofar as the first movement describes a circle whose radius is randomly larger than a single point.

19

At this point we might well ask what notion possessed the *nous* to impel a random material particle, chosen from that enormous number of points and to revolve it in whirling dance. And why this notion did not possess it earlier! To this, Anaxagoras would say, "*Nous* has the privilege of free random choice; it may start at random; it depends only on itself, whereas all other things are determined by something outside themselves. *Nous* has no duty and hence no purpose or goal which it would be forced to pursue. Having once started with its motion, and thus having set itself a goal, it would be . . ." To complete this sentence is difficult. Heraclitus did; he said, ". . . a game."

This seems to me to have been the final solution, the ultimate answer, that ever hovered on the lips of the Greeks. The Spirit of Anaxagoras is a creative artist. It is, in fact, the most tremendous mechanical and architectural genius, creating with the simplest means the most impressive forms and orbits, creating a movable architectonic, as it were, but ever from the irrational free random choosing that lies in the artist's depths. It is as though Anaxagoras were pointing to Phidias and—confronted by the enormous art object of the cosmos—were proclaiming as he would of the Parthenon, "Coming-to-be is not a moral but an esthetic phenomenon." Aristotle relates that Anaxagoras answered the question as to why human existence had value for him as follows: "Because it allows me to view the heavens and the whole order of the cosmos." He treated of physical things as reverently and with the same mysterious awe with which we stand before an antique temple. His doctrine became a sort of free-thinker's devotional exercise, protecting itself by means of the *odi profanum vulgus et arceo* and cautiously choosing its devotees from the highest, noblest Athenian society. In the exclusive community of the Athenian Anaxagorians, popular mythology was permitted only as a symbolic language. Among them, all the myths, all the gods, all the heroes, were taken to be but the hieroglyphics of nature-interpretation. Even the Homeric epic was to be the canonical song of the rule of *nous* and of the battles and laws of *physis*. Now and again a note sounded in this society of sublime free-thinkers would resound among the people. Particularly the great and always bold Euripedes, ever contemplating something new, dared to let several things out, under the disguise of the tragic mask, which arrow-like pierced the senses of the masses and from which they freed themselves only by farcical caricatures and ridiculous re-interpretations.

But the greatest Anaxagorian of them all was

Pericles, the mightiest and worthiest man on earth. As to him Plato testifies that only the philosophy of Anaxagoras gave his genius its sublime flight. When he stood before his people as public orator, in the beautiful rigidity and motionlessness of a marble Olympian and began to speak, calmly, wrapped in his mantle, its draperies unmoved, his countenance without change of expression, without smile, his strong voice powerfully even—when, totally different from Demosthenes, he spoke in his "Periclean" manner, thundering, flashing, destroying, redeeming—then he represented the very image of the Anaxagorian cosmos, the image of *nous* itself that has built for itself a most beautiful and worthy mansion. Pericles represented the visible human realization of the constructive, moving, distinguishing, ordering, reviewing, planning, artistically creative, self-determining power of the spirit. Anaxagoras himself once said that man is the wisest of beings, harboring a greater fullness of *nous* in himself than all the other creatures, if for no other reason than that he possesses such admirable organs as hands. He concluded therefore that *nous* according to the extent and mass by which it occupies a material body, always builds for itself out of the available material, tools suitable to the degree to which it appears. In other words, it constructs the most useful and beautiful organs wherever it appears in relatively greatest fullness. And just as the most miraculous and purposeful deed of *nous* had to be that wheeling primal motion, since just before it was made, spirit was still undividedly one, so surely the effect of a Periclean oration must often have seemed to the listening Anaxagoras a symbol of the primal revolution. For here too he felt first a whirl of thought, moving with orderly but terrifying force, gradually seizing, with its progressive spirals, first the near and then the far, taking them along and finally reaching its end by having re-formed the entire nation into a pattern of order and distinction.

To the later philosophers of antiquity, the way in which Anaxagoras used his *nous* to explain the world seemed strange, in fact hardly forgivable. It seemed to them as though he had found a magnificent tool but hadn't understood it right, and they sought to make up for what the finder had missed. In other words, they failed to recognize the meaning of Anaxagoras' renunciation, which had been the outcome of his truly pure scientific method, the method which in all cases and above all else asks not to what end something arises (*causa finalis*) but how something arises (*causa efficiens*). *Nous* was not dragged in by Anaxagoras to answer the specific questions, "how did motion come into being" or "how is it that there are regular motions." Yet Plato objects that he should have shown, but did not do so, that each thing in its own fashion and its own place is most beautifully, best, and usefully situated. But this Anaxagoras would have dared assert of no specific case; for him the available world was by no means the most perfect imaginable, for he saw everything arise from everything and found the segregation of substances by *nous* unaccomplished and imperfect, both so far as the end of filled space in the world is concerned, and so far as individual beings are concerned. It was perfectly sufficient for his insight to have found a motion which is capable of creating visible order in a thoroughly mixed chaos, by means of a simple continuous action. And he took good care to avoid asking as to the wherefore of motion, as to its reasonable purpose. For if the *nous* had to fulfill by means of its motion a purpose necessary to its nature, then its starting movement was no longer a matter of free choice. For insofar as *nous* is eternal, it would have been determined by its purpose eternally, and then there could have been no time when such motion was still lacking. It would have been logically forbidden, in fact, to assume a starting point for motion, in which case the conception of primeval chaos, the whole fundament of Anaxagoras' world interpretation, would likewise have been a logical impossibility. In order to escape such difficulties, always created by teleology, Anaxagoras always had to emphasize most strongly and with the greatest conviction that spirit has free, arbitrary choice. All its acts, including that of primal motion, are acts of "free will," he must say, whereas the entire remainder of the world grows under strict determination—mechanical determination in fact. But absolute free will can only be imagined as purposeless, roughly like a child's game or an artist's creative play-impulse. It is an error to ascribe to Anaxagoras the ordinary confusion of teleologists who in their admiration of the extraordinary efficiency, of the marvellous agreement of the parts with the whole particularly in the case of organisms, assume that whatever exists for the intellect originated with the intellect, and whatever the intellect manages to do under the guidance of purpose must also have been created in nature by thoughtfulness and a concept of purpose. (Schopenhauer, *Welt als Wille und Vorstellung,* Vol. II, Book 2, Chapter 26 on Teleology). Thinking in the style of Anaxagoras, on the contrary, suggests that the order and efficiency of things are but the direct result of blind mechanical movement. And only in order to produce such movement, in order to get past the dead inertia of chaos somehow, at some point in time, Anaxagoras assumed a free undetermined *nous,* dependent on itself alone. What he especially esteemed in it was its quality of randomness, hence its ability to activate unconditionally, undeterminedly, guided by neither causes nor ends.

Gateway Editions